JUDGING DOGS

JUDGING DOGS

R. H. Smythe, M.R.C.V.S.

JOHN GIFFORD LTD
119-125 CHARING CROSS ROAD
LONDON, WC2

First Published 1972 by
John Gifford Ltd
119-125 Charing Cross Road
London, WC2

SBN 70710382 7

Printed in Great Britain by
Compton Printing Ltd., London and Aylesbury

Contents

Introduction

In judging dogs as in judging human beings, justice must not only be done but it must be *seen* to be done. Exhibitors who fail to get their dogs placed are only too eager to blame everybody and everything apart from their dogs. It must be admitted that frequently this is not entirely the exhibitor's fault. Quite a percentage of exhibitors who show dogs would be quite incapable of placing the best three out of half-a-dozen of other owners' dogs, of their own particular breed; and, like fond mothers, they are capable only of seeing virtue in their own.

Every judge expects to be abused for his ignorance but there should never be any reason for him to be abused for not looking. In other words he* should go over every dog carefully seeking the good points as much as he seeks the faults. No owner will then be able to say his, or her dog 'was never looked at'. In the long run the results may be the same, for an experienced judge looking for the first time at a class of fifteen dogs can usually pick out five at a glance that he would never award cards to, if it could be avoided. Nevertheless, he should look these dogs over as conscientiously as the others. Occasionally, one is surprised when going over a very ordinary looking dog at close quarters, how closely it adheres to the standard, even if it lacks that little bit of 'personality' which catches the eye.

If the dog is given careful attention and goes out cardless, the handler will know that in the judge's opinion the exhibit is inferior to at least three others in the class and it is up to the

* From now onwards, when judges are concerned, for 'he' include 'she', as there are equally good judges in either se..

i

exhibitor, if he is not satisfied, to show again (and again, if need be) under other judges.

There is a possibility of a judge being *too* competent to give general satisfaction. He sees twenty or more dogs circling the ring. His eye focuses on one, three or five, as the case may be, but the others pass with scarcely a look from the judge, or so the handler thinks. He is probably wrong; the judge does look, though his attitude is one of a man walking along a pavement. He passes scores of persons without a glance and then *one* catches his eye, quite unavoidably it might appear; perhaps merely because he possesses an artistic eye, and can recognise real beauty immediately. It is not the job of the casual walker on the pavement to call in the less attractive individuals and find their faults and their good points but when the judge is in the ring at a dog show, he *must* do this. At any rate every exhibitor has paid an entry fee and he is entitled to some service for his money.

It is an unfortunate fact that many of our most popular judges have judged the same dogs before and that they recognise them again, and know their handlers, their owners and the status of the kennel from which they come.

We must try to believe that none of this knowledge influences our judge in the slightest and that he would have no hesitation in picking out a dog handled in amateur fashion by an entirely unknown youngster and placing it above the C.C. winner exhibited by one of the leading and wealthiest kennels. When one does this we must take our hats off to him — and hope he is right.

It is essential that every judge should know by heart the Breed Standard of each dog he judges, and that whether he approves or disapproves of the way the Standard is written, or compiled, he must abide by it until such time as the Standard is altered. I may have some respect for, but not complete faith in, the judge (and there are several) who declares, 'Standards! I never look at them. I reckon I know a good dog when I see one'.

The last man I heard say this judged a variety class immediately after. He found his first prize winner in an undersized

Pyrenean which had a frightfully hollow back. In his critique he wrote: 'I put her up on account of her vast amount of lung space'. By the Standard the Pyrenean is rather flat-sided.

He turned down a first-rate Bulldog on the grounds that it was unsound, cow-hocked, and turned its feet out. Had he read the Breed Standard he would have known that what would not go down in a Terrier may be exactly right in a Bulldog.

All of which goes to show that even if one is convinced that he knows a good dog when he sees one, if he is to make his awards in keeping with the accepted Standards, it is necessary that he should be familiar with their contents.

But it must not be supposed that a man who sat down for a twelvemonth to study and could recite the contents of every Standard by heart, could go into a ring, look through a class of fourteen Fox Terriers, or a variety class containing a dozen different breeds, and place them all in order of merit. Judging is not all that easy.

In the first place one who is to judge dogs must have lived among dogs, handled them and watched them moving, for a long time before he can apply all he has learned from the Standards. Nor is it possible, or at least likely, that if four experienced judges who *had* read the Standards, were asked to judge the same class of fourteen dogs of ten different varieties quite independently of one another, they would agree as to which were the three best dogs present, or if they did agree it is still improbable they would place them in the same order.

There are several reasons for this. Every breed has its own characteristics as represented in the Breed Standard. But, the Standard is not so precise that in a class of fourteen Labradors, for example, there might not be at least six at a Championship show which would meet every requirement in the Standard. How then does one discriminate?

The reason may be that every breed contains varying types. Specimens may be in show parlance, doggy, bitchy, coarse, fine, heavyweight, lightweight: and every judge, particularly the experienced one, will have his own particular likes and dislikes within the limits of these possible variations.

iii

Then again, take a Terrier breed for example; every specimen whether it be a Cairn or an Airedale has its own particular personality. (I know no better way of describing it.) And many good judges consider that a dog to win its class, must not only be sound and Standard-worthy but it must carry that representative aura, the hall-mark of its breed. All my readers may not grasp my meaning, but every experienced breeder and exhibitor will probably understand what I am trying to explain.

It follows therefore that one may show a dog before one particular judge and collect a C.C. but a week later before another equally sound and honest judge, the owner may in virtually the same company, have to be content with a third or fourth place. This need be no reflection on either judge. Each selected the type he fancied and as there was little between the first four exhibits the judge was perfectly entitled to follow his own likes and inclinations.

There is another point to remember. Dogs, like their owners, have their 'on' days and their 'off' days. They are enjoying themselves today or they may be bored stiff tomorrow, and the immediate environment may have a lot to do with this. Some dogs are better in the open, others seem to shine in the midst of discomfort and on a slippery floor. At a certain agricultural show I attended recently, the local brass band went into violent action just as the best in show was being selected. I feel sure in my own mind that the Miniature Poodle which shot off under the judge's table, was unlucky, and the Airedale who at once stood alertly at attention, had a great deal to be thankful for. That is typical of the sporting side of dog-showing and most exhibitors take it all in good part.

There are other considerations for the budding amateur who aspires to become a judge, to bear in mind. Inexperienced judges are apt to detect a fault, almost gleefully, and wipe the exhibit off the slate. He must not fail to look that same exhibit over very carefully and see what good points he can find which may outweigh the one fault. He need not fear that putting up a dog with a fault will lower him in the eyes of the exhibitors generally. In any case he will have a critique to write and he can always state the reasons for his actions.

iv

He will be lucky in his early days of judging if most of the dogs which come before him do not possess a lot of faults, so he had better find the good points too, and with a picture in his mind of the dog the Standard demands, endeavour to balance up the good with the bad and try to determine either which exhibit most nearly approaches the Standard — or, conversely, which departs from it the least.

Again, he must not forget to study his exhibit as a whole. A lot of judges, even the good ones we have with us today, are apt to pay too much attention to one part of the body. Some pay it to heads and overlook shoulders which are just as important. A few dote on feet, while others go all out for hocks and elbows. When all else fails, quite a number make a fetish of movement, which in itself might be quite a good thing, excepting that movement may be the greatest test of judging skill, and to be perfectly frank, not all judges excel in this direction. This is nobody's fault, for the reason that the gift of analysing movement is not given to all. The writer has been placed in a situation where for many years he had to award marks to students in examinations relating to soundness, and it has to be recognised that after several years training there are still intelligent individuals who are genetically *unable* to detect any abnormality of gait or determine the lame leg unless the animal is compelled to carry it. I am making this statement because experience has taught me that understanding movement and action is a gift not vouchsafed to everyone. It is like colour-blindness. Just as many have the one defect as the other, and in either case it is a reality: Incidentally, it affects members of both sexes.

The successful judge must be competent and honest, and although he must be courteous to every handler and kind in his handling of every exhibit, he must be completely deaf to everything the owner says to him, both while he is judging — and beforehand. For all practical purposes only the exhibit and the judge exist for their short space of time together. The other end of the lead does not matter. Any discussion between judge and owner must be carried on *after* the judging is finished.

I am fully aware that as the author of a book of this kind, I shall come under the usual degree of criticism. Let me say that at the moment I am concerned only with my subject and to everything else I am conveniently deaf.

My reason for writing is that at present we have more shows than judges and new judges have to be made to take their place in the next generation. They will be needed.

The great many of our present-day judges are past middle-age and although they are still 'with it', the day cannot be far away before a few of them will be content to sit at the ringside and somebody will have to replace them inside the ring.

We have far too few opportunities for training the young and it must be confessed that among the male element there are not so many aspirants and I can foresee the judges of twenty years ahead being 75% female, which may not be such a bad thing, judging from this present generation.

A few attempts at times are made to institute training classes for young people in the matter of judging, but the fact is that possible aspirants are so scattered that it is impracticable to get them into one place at a given time, which will enable them to get home perhaps twenty or thirty miles, after a lecture.

It would be a good thing if classes could be organised by those bodies who cater for extra-mural tuition to provide tuition at a number of centres. It might be considered worthwhile if the authorities could be made to understand that the Dog Fancy, with all its supporters and the existing registrations, is an important branch of industry, because whether we regard it as a hobby, sport or business, the Dog Fancy, annually, is responsible for a very considerable cash turnover, and in the public eye, that counts.

What it means to the breeder and owner is another matter. If their only inducement were cash, the Dog Fancy could come to an end tomorrow.

I agree fully with those who say that listening to lectures will not make a young person a judge. There would have to be an arrangement made with local kennels to permit parties of students to visit their kennels in company with a capable person, preferably an existing judge and compare specimens, good and bad, and learn the appropriate breed Standards. Once the ambition to become a judge has been instilled, then it is up to the candidate to make his or her way by working in kennels, visiting shows and attending more classes — if they can be provided.

Illustrations

ERRATA

List of Illustrations

27 Bones of the Feet *should read* page 63 not 65

28 The Top Lines *should read* page 68 not 78

47 Musterlander *should read* Münsterländer

Page 156

The Finnish Spity *should read* The Finnish Spitz

1

How dogs are judged

An experienced, capable judge, one blessed with a discerning eye, is generally able to assess the qualities of a dog of any familiar breed at a glance, or he, or she, will at least make a useful estimate of its potentialities within a matter of seconds.

The estimate will, of course, be the preliminary to a longer and closer examination in which not only the eyes but the hands and finger tips will each play a part. The judge will then bring into use some knowledge of surface anatomy with special reference to the layout of bones, joints and muscles hidden from view.

Many exhibits when first they enter the ring, may give an impression of being possible champions, mainly perhaps because they have been so carefully barbered and trained that their good points are emphasised and their imperfections neatly covered over.

The eye alone is not sufficient to reveal the truth and it would be easy to misjudge unless one possessed capable hands and a knowledge of the structures which lie beneath the skin.

This applies particularly to the long-coated breeds such as Poodles and Collies, Pekingese and Maltese, to quote a few examples.

A good handler can often make certain dogs look good merely by clipping or pulling out coat from some parts of the body and leaving it on other parts. But this is not so easy in the case of the smooth-coated breeds such as the Smooth Fox Terrier, apart from the fact that necks can be made to look longer by leaving coat where neck joins withers and hair may be left on the second thighs when these are not so well developed as one might wish. The experienced judge will proably admire the art of the handler in showing the dog to the best advantage, but will not be taken in by it. A novice might easily be deceived, especially one without any knowledge of surface anatomy, or one who has never learned to use the fingers in the way a judge *should* be able to do.

The judge at a dog show first sees his exhibits circling the ring in procession. If there are only a few entries in the class the task is simplified but when thirty or forty dogs of a variety of breeds are tumbling over one another, the matter is not so easy. In any case the slow walk is not a natural gait for any dog and one which cannot be practised in the open with all brakes on.

It usually succeeds in picking out the timid novices, two-legged and four-legged, and leaves the 'old hands' in possession, but this is not always an advantage.

One thing every judge *must* do, and this is examine every dog in the ring carefully even if it appears insignificant or a monstrosity. The owner has paid an entrance fee and has a right to a little of the judge's time.

It is to be expected that every 'all rounder' judge will know the Standards of every breed by heart.

When first looking over the individual dogs in a class, in order to gain an opinion as to its worth as an exhibit, it is a good plan to adopt a regular routine, working by numbers.

(1) Stance: Observe how the dog stands on its feet; the position of the head, and the dog's general demeanour.

(2) Decide whether male or female; and in the former case, whether entire. By recent changes in K.C. rules a unilateral cryptorchid may now be exhibited but a testicular abnormality must be regarded as a fault.

(3) Head and ear carriage.

(4) Colour of eyes; and in certain breeds, colour of eye rims. The size and shape of the eye and amount of eyeball visible. The presence or absence of entropion.

(5) Shape and colour of nose.

(6) Whether obviously undershot or overshot. Presence of premolars and general regularity of incisors.

(7) Size, shape and position of ears.

(8) Relative lengths of cranium and foreface. Presence or absence of the 'stop'. Development of brows.

(9) Length of neck, and its relation to shoulders and breast. Head carriage.

(10) Degree of shoulder inclination, and whether the shoulder carries excessive muscle.

(11) Spring of ribs and depth of chest. The degree of rib curvature required differs in various breeds.

(12) The body-coupling, i.e. the length between the last (floating) rib and the outer angle of the pelvis.

(13) Length of back; topline and quarters.

(14) Set-on and length of tail, and how carried.

(15) The forelimbs. How set into body; length and straightness. Type of bone. Position and shape of elbows.

(16) The hindlimbs. Stifles and hocks; degree of angulation.

(17) Pasterns and feet.

(18) Coat. Thickness of skin. Degree of wrinkling. Throatiness. Presence or absence of dewlap.

(19) *Movement and Temperament.*

The last, but far from the least. Movement is always of the greatest importance, and the style is different in many breeds. Always pay heed to the Standard in cases in which the movement is specified in any particular breed of dog.

Movement requires a chapter to itself.

It is not always easy to judge temperament at a glance, especially on the 'first time out'. Any dog that is deliberately aggressive towards other exhibits or the judge should be penalised. Of late years there has been a tendency to place conformation first, and when this was excellent, to overlook faulty temperament. Today it is becoming more and more apparent that this has been a mistake. Not infrequently the members of breeds noted for their friendliness have become unreasonably aggressive.

2

Some thoughts on anatomy

Canine anatomy is much too wide a subject to discuss in any details in a book of this kind, but there are some elementary aspects of it, which every judge should know.

The position and names of the various bones can be learned from the accompanying illustration.

THE HEAD

From the viewpoint of judging there are three varieties of heads met with in dogs, together with some intermediate types. In some instances crossing has taken place tween two diverse types (long and short) and the progeny have again been mated to an intermediate type, or to another of the two diverse types. The consequence is that there are now in existence several hundred breeds, none of which possess heads similar in every detail.

The three principal types are:

(a) The *dolichocephalic,* or long-head. This has an elongated cranium and long jaw bone, the upper and lower of which are commonly of equal length.

(b) The *brachycephalic,* or short-head. In this type the cranial portion of the skull is normal in size, or proportionately a little more capacious, but the jaws are short, and in a number of instances the lower jaw is a little longer than the upper, giving rise to an 'undershot' mouth.

As the nasal bones are much shortened, the sense of smell is less acute and there may be difficulty in breathing.

In the dolichocephalic breeds the eyes are situated a little obliquely, slightly towards the side of the head so that bifocal vision is difficult to attain, except at long range.

4

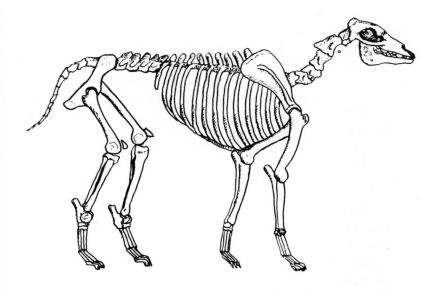

Fig. 1   Skeleton of a Pointer

In the brachycephalic dogs such as the Bulldog, Pekingese and Pug, the eyes are nearly as frontally placed as our own, and bifocal vision is much more easily made use of. In the short-headed dogs the amount of cornea exposed between the eyelids is usually greater than in the long-headed varieties.

(c) The mesocephalic breeds have probably been produced by crossbreeding between the long and short-headed varieties. This was not so likely in days long past since the long heads were hunters and lived outdoors, but the short heads had no well-developed jaws and lived on vegetable material, and probably on human refuse, or human charity. They were un-doubtedly the first 'pets', and possibly a few from each litter were reared and fattened until they were ready to roast. The two varieties probably met but seldom, and interbreeding was

5

not common. It is likely that the brachycephalic breeds were mutations, from the long-headed varieties.

A few breeds appear to be intermediate between the meso-cephalic and the brachycephalic. The shape of the skull and cranium in such instances is mainly mesocephalic in that the bones at the base of the skull are developed better than in the purely brachycephalic breeds, but the jaws are a little longer and usually there is rather less tendency to being undershot.

Such breeds include the Cavaliers, Apsos, Tibetan Spaniel and the Tibetan Terrier.

A few breeds appear to lie between the mesocephalic and dolichocephalic. These may carry a variable proportion of brachycephalic blood.

Examples are the Mastiff, Boxer, Papillon and Chihuahua.

The dolichocephalic group embraces all the gundogs, including Pointers, Weimeraners, Retrievers and Spaniels but not the Tibetan Spaniel or the true King Charles. Also among the long heads are the Hound Group, and members of the Working group (apart from the Boxer), the Dalmatian, Keshond, the Poodles and Schnauzer. Examples of the Mesocephalics are Boston Terrier, Bullmastiff and the Boxer, although as previously stated, the latter appears to carry a rather greater share of the dolichocephalic strain.

Among the brachycephalics we may include the Griffon Bruxellois, Japanese, King Charles, Pekingese, Pug, Bulldog, French Bulldog, Shih Tzu and the Apso, though the latter shows more of the mesocephalic type than the Shih Tzu, as is indicated by slightly greater length of muzzle.

From the viewpoint of judging, all heads are different, but they have, all of them, a certain number of structures in their composition.

The influence of these varies in every skull according to their degree of development, quite irrespective of all the fixed features such as cranium, foreface and jaws.

The structures which can so greatly vary the appearance of the head, even that of a typical brachycephalic head are:
(a) The zygoma and zygomatic arch.
(b) The occiput.

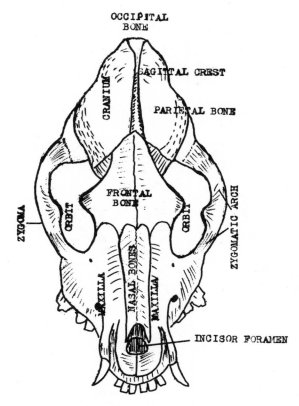

OCCIPITAL
BONE

SAGITTAL CREST

CRANIUM

PARIETAL BONE

ORBIT

FRONTAL
BONE

ORBIT

ZYGOMA

ZYGOMATIC ARCH

MAXILLA

NASAL BONES

MAXILLA

INCISOR FORAMEN

Fig. 2   Skull of Bullmastif (Mesocephalic)

(c) The sagittal crest.

(d) The orbit.

(e) The degree of development of the frontal sinuses, which
     are responsible for the depth and appearance of the 'stop'.

The *cranium* (the brain box) remains fairly constant in shape
although it varies in capacity in different breeds, with a tendency for it to be considerably larger in its relative proportion
to the bodyweight in the short-faced dogs than in the long-
headed varieties.

At the uppermost extremity of the cranium is *the occipital
bone* which is large in some breeds and small in others. It is this
bone which provides the large 'peak' in such as the Basset

7

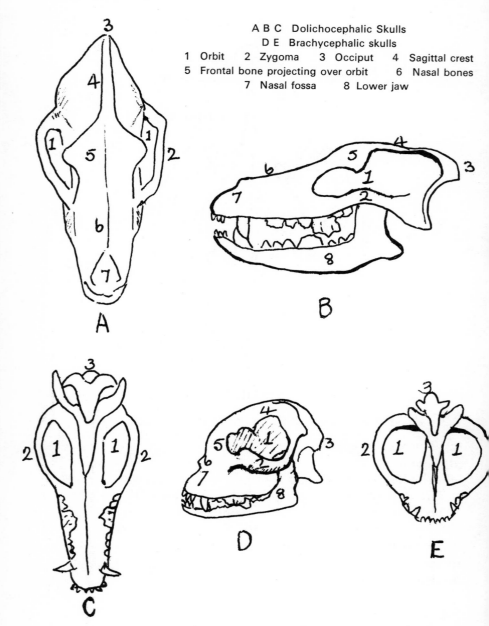

A B C Dolichocephalic Skulls
D E Brachycephalic skulls
1 Orbit 2 Zygoma 3 Occiput 4 Sagittal crest
5 Frontal bone projecting over orbit 6 Nasal bones
7 Nasal fossa 8 Lower jaw

Fig. 3 Skulls of Dogs

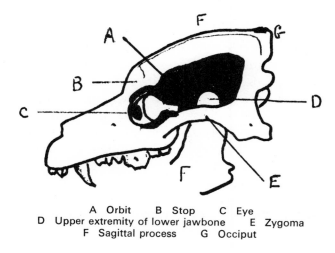

A   Orbit   B   Stop   C   Eye
D   Upper extremity of lower jawbone   E   Zygoma
F   Sagittal process   G   Occiput

Fig. 4   Skull seen from the side

Hound and Bloodhound. It is very evident in the Field Spaniel and the Clumber, but not in the Springer, nor is it markedly prominent in the Cocker. It is well developed in the Hounds generally, including the Afghan, but only just visible in the Borzoi.

Although so obvious in the Basset hound it is not prominent in the Beagle, Greyhound and Whippet.

Another feature which markedly affects the shape of the cranial portion of the skull is a ridge of bone, present along the middle line of the head, running longitudinally from between the occiput to as far down as the upper part of the 'stop'. It is termed the *sagittal crest*. The presence of this ridge of bone leaves a depression on either side of it, known as the *temporal fossa* and this depression is filled by the temporal muscles which help to close the jaws, and play their part in mastication. When the sagittal crest is *high* and the temporal muscle *moderately* developed, the cranium will be fairly well defined, as in the Bedlington or the Borzoi.

9

When the ridge is *moderately* high and the temporal muscles *well* developed, the forehead will be wide, as in the Labrador.

In the Fox Terriers the sagital crest is relatively high, more so than in the Labrador, but the temporal muscles are less prominent with the result that the forehead appears to be raised throughout its length right down its central portion, falling away on either side to produce a long, narrow head, the impression being made more manifest by the narrowness and straightness of the *zygoma*, which we will discuss presently.

The sagittal crest is less prominent in the brachycephalic breeds in which the *zygomatic arch* is well-developed, with the upper part of the skull wide and rounded, or sometimes flat between the ears, as in the Pekingese.

The Zygoma and Zygomatic Arch

The zygoma is a bone, shaped like a semicircle, present on either side of the head, prominent in every brachycephalic skull.

It is present also in the dolichocephalic, long-headed, and narrow skull, but in this case instead of being a semicircle, the bone runs close alongside the side of the skull without forming a distinct arch.

It is the zygoma alone which decides how wide the head will be. A very wide head contains no bigger cranium and no more brain than a narrow one, possibly less. The difference depends entirely upon the width of the zygomatic arch.

Within the semicircle of the zygomatic arch lie two important structures. The front portion of the arch contains the

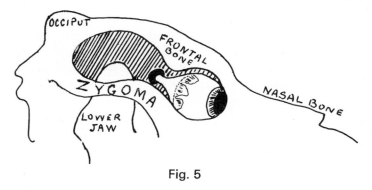

Fig. 5

eye, within a cavity known as the *orbit*. Behind the eye at the hinder end of the zygomatic arch lies the *articulation of the jaw* and the *upper end of the lower jawbone*.

The zygoma is the main factor in the design of the head of every dog. It will determine for example, whether a Fox Terrier will carry a lean, fine head without undue cheek, or if it will have a coarse skull, which will throw it completely out of the reckoning, quite irrespective of all the virtues it may possess elsewhere.

Incidentally, the zygoma gives attachment to the *masseter muscle*, a solid very powerful mass in some breeds, such as the Bull Terrier. Its purpose is to give strength to the grip between the jaws, but the Fox Terrier is required to snap in order to kill, and not to crunch and hold on as the Bull Terrier does, and so, in the former, the zygoma must run parallel with the side of the head and it must not carry a very heavy masseter muscle. The Bull Terrier has well developed masseter muscles which provide the 'cheeks'.

The frontal *sinuses* are two cavities in the frontal bone, one on either side of the centre of the head immediately above the eyes. The cavities communicate with the air passages travelling through the nostrils. These cavities vary in different breeds. Their bony covering gives origin to the 'brows', and the cavity between them, as it joins up with the nasal bones which lie at a slightly lower level, forms the 'stop'.

The *stop* is regarded as a very essential character in some breeds but it must be absent or ill-defined in others. It should be prominent in the Boxer, the gundogs and in most of the hounds; but absent in the Greyhound and Whippet.

It will be shallow in a Saluki, but deep in a Bullmastiff or a Chihuahua and absent in the continuous line down the head of the 'downfaced' Bull Terrier. It is only slightly developed in the Alsatian, Bearded Collie, Rough Collie, Dobermann and Great Dane.

In the Pekingese the stop is characteristically deep as it is also in the Shih Tzu.

The stop seldom appears in puppies before they are nine or ten weeks old.

The purpose of the frontal sinuses has long been misunderstood. Originally it was believed that they were concerned with the sense of smell but they do not carry the sensitive areas required for the detection of odours, and, moreover, air enters them during expiration and *not* during inspiration. Their real purpose is to enlarge the head at an important part without requiring an excessive amount of bone to accomplish it, so keeping down the weight (see Figs. 4 and 5).

The *orbit* in the dog is an open *cavity*, not *closed* around the eyeball as in the horse, ox, sheep or pig. Some attempt has been made to close it by the outgrowth of a small piece of bone from the edge of the frontal bone. From this a ligament passes between the upper and lower margins of the zygomatic bone and the frontal bone.

The eye is contained in the front portion of this cavity, with the coronoid process of the upright portion of the lower jaw in the hinder section.

The zygomatic arch may be felt quite clearly with the fingertips and its width estimated.

In the Bulldog the tips of the fingers should almost enter the space between zygoma and cranium, whereas in a Fox Terrier the zygoma should lie close to and almost parallel with the side of the cranium, leaving room for a small eye only, or at any rate for only a narrow *palpebral orifice* between the upper and lower eyelids.

SKULLS IN CERTAIN BREEDS
The Head

Every judge pays a great deal of attention to the head, and for a very good reason.

The head has a large number of special features and the degree in which each of these is developed produces a variety of combinations present in each particular breed.

Among these variable characteristics we may include:

(a) Absence or presence of an occiput.

(b) The shape of the forehead, whether flat, rounded, wide or narrow according to the degree of development of the sagittal crest, the width of the zygomatic arch and the development of the muscles which lie in the fossae over-lying the parietal bones.

(c) The width of the zygomatic arch completely decides the shape of the head. It may be narrow and flat-sided as in the Fox Terrier, or wide and flat as in the Labrador, or comparatively narrow but somewhat domed as in the Cocker Spaniel.

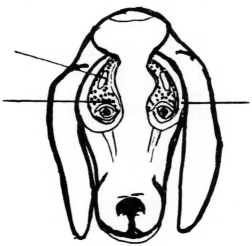

Fig. 6   Diagram of Head of Cocker
Showing the position and curvature of the zygomatic arch. The orbital cavity is dotted. It contains the eyeball and the upper end of the lower jaw.

The head may be apple-domed as in the Chihuahua, or round and without indentation as in the Pug; or broad, wide and flat between the ears as in the Pekingese.

(d) The ears are characteristic in nearly every breed and vary enormously in size, shape and disposition.

(e) The stop gives indication as to the degree of development of the frontal sinuses and it divides the head into two parts. In every breed the relationship between the portion of the head above the stop and that below it down as far as the tip of the nose, alters the facial appearance and expression. Heads are thus divided into dolichocephalic (long) mesocephalic (medium) and brachycephalic (short-faced).

13

(f) The facial index denotes the angle that exists between the two portions, that above and below the stop.

In some breeds, the outline of the head above and below the site of the stop may be continuous as in the Borzoi in which the stop is not perceptible and there is inclination towards a 'Roman nose'.

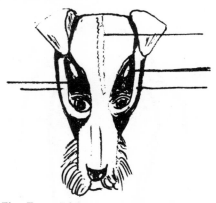

Fig. 7   Diagram of Terrier Head
Showing position of zygoma beneath skin, almost devoid of curvature, and eye in orbit.

In the Bull Terrier the profile curves gently downwards from the top of the skull to the tip of the nose, the head is long with all the normal indentations filled (downfaced), but in the Staffordshire Bull Terrier the head is long with a broad skull and a distinct stop, with very pronounced cheek muscles. In the Terriers which kill by snapping rather than by hard biting, the cheek muscles are not prominent.

In the brachycephalic breeds there may be little foreface, but a comparatively large skull.

(g) The jaws are usually characteristic for the breed and may be level, overshot or undershot. The lower jaw may be straight or it may curve upwards, as in the Bulldog.

(h) The lips vary in different breeds according to whether they meet in line or overlap as in the Bulldog, in which the upper 'flews' drop over the lower lips. To show the incisor teeth is invariably a fault.

14

Fig. 8   Head of Cocker Spaniel

(i) The length and width of the upper jaw and whether the jaws are square or tapering. The colour of the nose is important.

(j) The apparent size and position of the eyes, almost frontally-placed in the brachycephalic breeds and slightly obliquely in most of the long-headed breeds. The depth at which the eyes are set may depend upon the amount of fat at the back of the eyeball. This may vary in the same individual according to bodily condition. The colour of the eyes is important. Usually they should be dark but exceptions may be found in the various Standards.

A consideration of the above possible differences will convince the reader that in the dog more than in any other living species there may be enormous variations, most of which have been introduced through centuries of selective breeding.

The consequence is that the expert can recognise any breed by its head alone and slight variations of the head in each

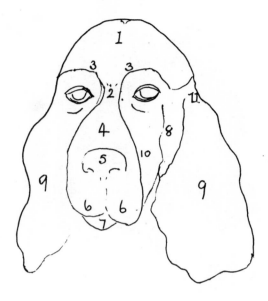

Fig. 8A   Parts of the Head of Cocker Spaniel

breed may decide whether a dog may be a winner or an 'also-ran'.

THE HEAD AND THE STANDARDS

The Standard of every breed devotes considerable space to a description of the head, and as the head is capable of a great deal more variation, generally, than any other part of the dog, judges need to study this very carefully.

The following notes will refer generally only to a few of the breeds, notably Gundogs and Terriers, emphasising features characteristic in each of these.

Gundogs

English Setter

Head long and lean, with well defined stop. Oval from ear to ear with prominent occiput. Flews not too pendulous. Stop to occiput and stop to nose equal in length.

Ch. Luna Star of Yadnum.
Owner: Ethel Munday.

Below
IRISH WOLFHOUND
Ch. Edgcroft Simon.
Owner: Mrs. Zena Andrews.

Dreamboat of Lochnell.

Ch. Ronlyn Miss Irrella.

Ch. Tahawi Belinda (Junior Warrant).

Gordon Setter

Head broader than muzzle and broadest between ears. Well-defined stop. Length from occiput to stop rather greater than from stop to nose. Muzzle not as deep as its length.

Irish Setter

Head long and lean, oval but not wide between ears. Marked occiput. Brows raised with obvious stop. Muzzle fairly deep and square. Longest from stop to nose; flews not pendulous.

Pointer

Skull of medium breadth. Skull horizontal with distinct stop. Muzzle square at end and slightly concave on upper surface (slightly dished face). Pronounced occiput.

German Short-haired Pointer

Face not dished. Prominent eyebrows. Nasal bone rises gradually from nose to forehead with no definite stop unless viewed from the side. Occiput not pronounced.

Retriever (Flat-Coated)

Skull flat, moderately broad. Head long. Stop gradual rather than accentuated with fairly prominent brows. Never dished or down-faced. Long strong jaws.

Retriever (Golden)

Broad skull with evident stop. Wide powerful muzzle.

Retriever (Labrador)

Clean cut head, broad forehead with pronounced stop. Skull and forehead parallel with foreface at a slightly lower level. Wide nose. Jaws nearly as long as skull and never snipy. Cheeks never prominent.

Spaniel (Clumber)

Head broad on top, large, square and massive, with decided occiput. Heavy brows with deep stop. Heavy muzzle with pronounced flews. Nose square and flesh-coloured. Eyes dark amber and slightly sunken. Ears large vine-leaf, hanging forward and with hair not extending past leathers.

Spaniel (Cocker)

Skull finely chiselled and domed or convex across top. Ears set low with fringed leathers. Cheek bones flattened. Distinct stop. Wide deep muzzle. Skull and muzzle equal in length. Eyes dark, full but not prominent.

Spaniel (Springer)

Skull medium length, fairly broad and slightly rounded, higher than foreface with pronounced stop. Fluting between eyes extending a short way along forehead. Cheeks flat. Muzzle fairly broad and deep without being coarse. Ears low set in line with eye, lobular and widest at ends.

Weimeraner

Head moderately long, clean cut and aristocratic with fluting between eyes carried back over forehead. Moderate stop, the head equal in length before and behind it. Prominent occiput. Forehead quite straight with tight skin. Powerful jaw.

American Cocker

Skull well-developed and moderately rounded at dome. Smooth forehead without wrinkles. Fluting from well-defined stop extending half-way up crown. Well-chiselled eye sockets with round full eyeballs looking directly forward, giving the eye a slightly almond-shaped appearance.

Distance from nose tip to stop should be half that from stop up over the crown to the base of skull. Muzzle broad, deep with square even jaws. Upper lips covering lower jaw squarely.

Ears lobular, set well back, at lower eye level, extending to nostrils, heavily fringed.

Terrier Group

Airedale

Skull long, flat, not too broad between ears, narrowing slightly to the eyes. Skull and forehead equal in length. Free from wrinkles, no very evident stop. Forehead filled below eyes. Strong foreface without prominent cheeks. Lips tight.

Bedlington Terrier

Skull narrow, deep and rounded. Outline slightly convex. Profuse, light-coloured silky topknot. No stop. Long tapering jaw. Well filled below eye, close fitting lips without flews. Small bright, well sunk eyes. Ears set low, filbert shaped, hanging flat on cheek, silvery fringe at tip.

Border Terrier

Head like that of an otter, moderately broad in skull with a short strong muzzle.

Bvll Terrier

Long, strong, deep right to end of muzzle, but not coarse. From the front appears egg-shaped without indentations. Profile curves gently downward from top of skull to (and including) nose tip. Strong underjaw. Eyes narrow, triangular and obliquely placed. Eyes nearer to tip of skull than to the nose.

Cairn Terrier

Skull broad, not too large, with a strong but not a heavy jaw. Decided indentation between eyes. Hair full on forehead.

Fox Terrier Smooth

Skull flat and moderately narrow, gradually decreasing in width to the eyes. Flat cheeks. Not much stop. Filled below eyes. A dip in profile between forehead and upper jaw.

Fox Terrier Wire

Skull flat on top, width decreasing towards eyes. Well developed jaw bones with strong white teeth. Flat cheeked.

Kerry Blue Terrier

Flattened long, lean skull. Slight stop. Foreface and jaw very strong, deep and punishing.

Lakeland Terrier

Skull flat and refined. Broad muzzle, not too long. Length of jaw from stop down, must not exceed length of skull from stop to occiput.

Norfolk Terrier

Skull fairly wide between ears, slightly rounded. Muzzle slightly less than half length of skull. Ears drooping.

Norwich Terrier

Muzzle foxy and strong, length one third less than from stop to occiput. Wide below ears and slightly rounded. Ears erect.

Scottish Terrier

Skull long but appearing narrow. Cheekbones flat. Slight but distinct stop. Prominent eyebrows. Ears fine, pointed, erect. The nose is large and the profile from nose to the chin below, appears to slope slightly backwards.

Sealyham Terrier

Skull slightly domed. Wide between ears. Powerful, long, square jaws. Slightly convex in outline, nose to occiput.

Staffordshire Bull Terrier

Short, deep through, broad skull. Very pronounced cheek muscles. Short foreface. Distinct stop. Mouth level, neither undershot nor overshot.

Welsh Terrier

Head flat, and rather wider than in Fox Terrier. Jaw a little deeper and more powerful than in Fox Terrier and ears set slightly more to the side though still directed forwards. Stop not too defined.

West Highland White

Skull slightly domed. Foreface slightly shorter than skull. Distinct stop and bony ridges above eye. Foreface well made-up beneath eyes and a distinct indentation between eyes. Ears small, erect and pointed. Head and face carrying a great amount of hair.

Bulldog

Skull very large. Viewed from the front very high from corner of lower jaw to top of skull. Cheeks well rounded and wide. Head very high but short between its back and tip of nose.

Forehead flat with loose wrinkled skin. Prominent projections on frontal bones cause a wide deep stop. From this a

Fig. 9   The Author's impression of a Bulldog's head as drawn from the description in the Standard.

furrow extends up to middle of skull. Muzzle short, broad, lower jaw longer and turned upwards. Very deep from corner of eye to corner of mouth. Flews, broad, broad thick and pendant quite covering the teeth. Two halves of lower jaw must be symmetrical and teeth normally placed.

French Bulldog

Head massive, square and broad. Flat between ears with domed forehead covered with wrinkled skin. Stop well defined. Lower jaw deep, square, broad, slightly undershot and turned upwards. Upper lip covers lower lip on each side without

Fig. 10   French Bulldog and Boston Terrier
Showing differences in head.

hanging too low. Teeth must not show. Muzzle broad, deep and laid well-back with well-developed cheek muscles. Eyes frontally placed, should show no white when looking forward.

Bat ears, wide at the base, rounded tip; erect and parallel.

Boston Terrier

Skull square, flat on top, free from wrinkles. Cheeks flat. Muzzle short, wide, square, and deeper than long. Free from wrinkles. Chops deep but not pendulous, covering the teeth when mouth is closed.

THE MOUTH

It is an unfortunate provision of nature in many cases that the lower jaw decides, as it nearly always does, to go on growing a little while after growth of the upper jaw has ceased.

This sometimes terminates in a slightly undershot jaw which ruins all prospect of winning in a number of breeds.

Nevertheless, an undershot jaw (in varying degrees), is present and quite acceptable in certain breeds.

Sometimes the lower teeth are expected to show but in most breeds they must be invisible and concealed beneath closely fitting lips.

Below is a table showing what is expected in different breeds with short faces:

Griffon Bruxellois	Slightly undershot. Lips close regularly over teeth.
Japanese	A wide mouth, neither undershot nor overshot.
Cavalier	Mouth square, wide and deep, well turned-up. The lips cover teeth and meet in line.
Pekingese	Mouth level. Lips meet. Must not show teeth or tongue.
Pug	Mouth short, square and level. *Not* upfaced.
Boston	Mouth even or slightly undershot. Muzzle short, square, wide and deep, without turn-up.
Bulldog	Muzzle short and broad with distinct turn-up of lower jaw. Considerably undershot. The two jaws must be parallel without 'wry mouth'. Six canines above and below in level line. Teeth should not be visible with mouth closed.
French Bulldog	Slightly undershot and well turned-up. Teeth regular and not visible with mouth closed. Tongue should not protrude.
Shih Tzu	Muzzle square and short. Mouth level or only *slightly* undershot. Should not show teeth when mouth is closed.
Tibetan Apso	Medium length muzzle. Level or slightly undershot. Muzzle *not* square but longer than that of Shih Tzu.

Tibetan   Slightly undershot. Teeth must not show when
  Spaniel mouth is closed.
Tibetan   Mouth preferably level but not penalised if slightly
  Terrier undershot.
Boxer   Length of muzzle compared with whole of head
            as 1:3.
            Lower edge of upper lip rests on upper edge of
            lower lip. Under jaw bent upwards to protrude
            slightly beyond upper jaw. Normally undershot.
Bullmastiff Slightly undershot, maybe, but level preferred.
            Lower jaw straight and *not* turned up.

DENTITION

Normally the dog has 42 teeth which include 6 incisors, above and below (12), 4 canines, 4 premolars, top and bottom on each side (16) and 10 molars.

In some of the small pointed mouths, notably in Toy Poodles, there may not be room for 6 incisors above and below, but on the other hand, there may be a double row, not necessarily complete, which is a grave fault.

In Bulldogs and Boxers, there may be 7 incisors in the upper jaw, or even 8, which is quite wrong. In Boxers the extra incisors produce a square jaw but they should be penalised.

It has been observed that Boxers with extra incisors may be subject to bone disorders, in the forelimbs especially.

The examination of the mouth and teeth is essential in the case of each exhibit. It is wise to wear rubber gloves and wash after handling each exhibit.

Opening the mouth may be carried out by the judge, or the handler may be requested to perform this part of the operation. There is less danger of carrying infection if the handler can cooperate but unless a judge is very careful, the thumb or fingers of the former may accidentally, or purposely, cover a fault. An exhibition dog should be trained so that its mouth can be opened by a stranger but the reverse is only too often the case.

The incisor teeth can be examined by placing the thumb and fingers of the left hand around the muzzle so that the dog can-not snap, whilst the fingers of the right hand gently raise and

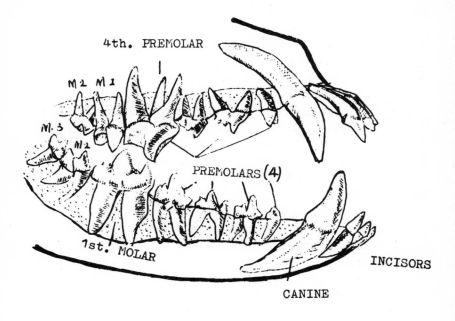

4th. PREMOLAR

M 2 M 1

M. 3

M 2

PREMOLARS (4)

1st. MOLAR

INCISORS

CANINE

Fig. 11 The complete set of teeth in the dog numbers 42

lower the lips. Teeth can be counted and examined for place-ment in this way.

The premolars (four on either side in each jaw), are not so easily seen but a repetition of the holding the muzzle closed with the left hand may enable the angle of the lips to be drawn back sufficiently for the molars and premolars to be examined and counted.

Opening the mouth may be necessary but should be avoided if possible. Opening the mouth is a knack. A veterinary sur-geon may open a hundred mouths and escape being bitten but the novice will be lucky if he does likewise.

Incisor teeth in every breed should number six above and below. In Bulldogs it is not extremely rare to find an extra tooth above, below or in both places, while in Boxers seven teeth above are fairly common and in some kennels this is even encouraged as it gives greater width to the jaw.

Nevertheless, extra teeth must be considered a fault and although many Boxers with an extra tooth win consistently, the fault should be penalised, not to the extent of throwing the exhibit out but by paying attention to it when making awards where an exhibit nearly as good possesses also a perfect mouth.

In Bulldogs the same may apply unless there are eight incisors, when it may be left to the experienced judge to do what he or she thinks best. The respective Standards specify the number (6) of incisors in either breed.

In Poodles, there should be all the premolars present and the Standards specify that a full mouth of 42 teeth is desirable.

In some breeds, particularly in Poodles, the premolars may be short in number or missing altogether. This must be heavily penalised — in spite of the fact that in prehistoric remains of dogs there is evidence that the premolars were absent in many skulls.

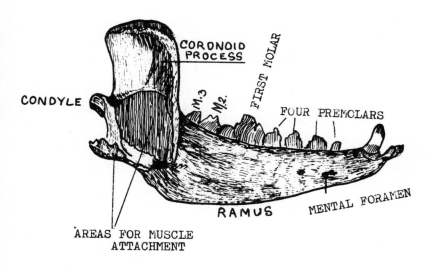

Fig. 12   Lower jaw of Dog

Missing teeth, due to pyorrhoea or caries, must be penalised, but when a tooth has apparently been knocked out by accident, the absence could be overlooked. This would apply only to a mouth perfect in other respects.

25

From the judge's viewpoint mouth faults come under three main headings:

(1) The overshot or undershot mouth.
(2) The wry mouth.
(3) Dentition.

In the majority of breeds of the long-headed variety the recognised association of the upper and lower incisors is the 'scissor bite', in which the upper incisors slightly overlap the lower so that the edges of the upper reach down about a quarter of the length of the lower incisors. If the upper incisors actually cover the lower teeth completely, then the dog is *overshot* which is a bad fault.

Conversely, the lower jaw may be too long as compared with the upper jaw so that the upper incisors, when the mouth is closed, lie behind the lower incisors. This is a very bad fault in the long-headed breeds but is accepted or demanded in some of the short-faced varieties.

The tendency is for the lower jaw to continue to grow a little while after growth in the upper jaw has ceased, so if one were judging a ten-months puppy and the lower incisors were level with, or very slightly underlapping, one would view the situation with a great deal of suspicion as to the final outcome. However one judges on the day with no attempt to be a prophet!

LEVEL MOUTH	SCISSOR BITE	UNDERSHOT
Italian Greyhound	Chow Chow	Boston Terrier
Manchester Terrier	Dalmatian	(Even or under-
Australian Terrier	Keeshond	shot, to square
Cairn	Poodle	muzzle)
Skye Terrier	Schnauzer	Bulldog
Welsh Terrier	All the Terrier	
Field Spaniel	Group not	French Bulldog
Clumber Spaniel	included under	(slightly)
Curly Coated Retriever	Level mouth	
Irish Setter	Basenji	Shih Tzu
Gordon Setter	Basset Hound	(Level or slightly
English Setter	(or level)	underhung)
Afghan	Bloodhound	
Borzoi	Dachshund	Tibetan Apso
Deerhound	Greyhound	(as Shih Tzu)
Rhodesian Ridgeback	Whippet	
Saluki	German Short-haired	Tibetan Terrier

LEVEL MOUTH	SCISSOR BITE	UNDERSHOT
Bearded Collie	Pointer	(as Shih Tzu)
Great Dane	Labrador Retriever	
Old English Sheepdog	Cocker Spaniel	Boxer
St. Bernard	Weimeraner	
Cardigan Corgi	American Cocker	Bullmastiff
Schipperke	Alsatian	(slightly or
Golden Retriever		level)
English Water Spaniel		Mastiff
Irish Water Spaniel	Rough Collie	(slightly — or
Welsh Springer	Dobermann	level
	Rottweiler	as Bullmastiff)
Sussex Spaniel	Samoyed	Griffon Bruxellois
	Shetland Sheepdog	
Welsh Corgi	Chihuahua	
Japanese	Maltese (or level)	
Cavalier King Charles	Miniature Pinscher	
Pekingese	Papillon	
Pomeranian	Newfoundland	
Yorkshire Terrier		

Breeds whose teeth are not mentioned in their Standards include: Pyrenean Mountain Dog, Pug, Beagle, Elkhound, Finnish Spitz, Foxhound, Irish Wolfhound, Pointers, Flatcoated Retriever.

THE EARS

Ear placement and ear carriage are of great importance when estimating the virtues of a show dog, and when comparing one exhibit with another. They are on many occasions the primary deciding cause as to whether a dog should be 'best in show', or among the 'also rans'.

In some breeds, as in the Terriers, a fairly good idea may often be obtained (if one has had some experience) of how ears will finish when growth of the puppy is complete. In other breeds, however, notably in Alsatians and Corgis, ears may be erect at three months; or one may be erect while the other 'flops'. It is said that in most prick-eared breeds no final decision can be arrived at before teething is over, but as this coincides approximately with the age of six months, one might regard this as the time to expect the ears to attain their permanent position.

Flop ears in Alsatians may be due to a variety of causes, mainly hereditary. The commonest is excess of skin, particularly in the region of the neck, while in some instances it is the

27

FOX TERRIER

WELSH TERRIER

SEALYHAM

W. H. WHITE

MANCHESTER TERRIER

BULL TERRIER

NORFOLK TERRIER

NORWICH TERRIER

SCOTTISH TERRIER

CAIRN

BASENJI

CHIHUAHUA

AIREDALE

COLLIE

O.E. TERRIER

ALSATIAN

Fig. 13   Ears

actual thickness of the skin of the ear alone which overweighs and overbalances the ear.

Alternatively, a very thin skin may reduce support to the ear cartilage, but the 'thick' ear is the more common offender.

Below is a list of the ears, as seen in various breeds:

Fox Terrier   Small and of moderate thickness. V-shaped. Their top line above skull level, the ear neatly folded over and falling forward.
Constantly alert to sound and movement.

Welsh Terrier   Small and V-shaped and slightly heavier than in the Fox Terrier, and also with a little more space between them, bringing them a little more obliquely towards the outer side of the head, without in any way tending to tip over the side.

West Highland White   Small, erect and terminating in a sharp point. Velvety skin without excess of hair (which should *not* be trimmed).

Sealyham   Ears medium in size, slightly rounded at tips and carried at side of cheeks.

Staffordshire Bull Terrier   Rose or half-pricked; not large. Never either fully dropped or fully pricked.

White Bull Terrier   Small, thin and close together. Stiffly erect and facing straight forward.

Scottish Terrier   Thin ears, pointed and fully erect.

Norfolk Terrier   V-shaped, rounded at tip and falling forward close to cheek.

Norwich Terrier   Ears erect.

Cairn Terrier   Ears erect, small and pointed, with plenty of space between them but not carried too far to the side of the head.

Airedale   Ears not too large with their top lines folded above skull level. Somewhat as in the Welsh Terrier, falling a *little* more outwardly than in the Fox Terriers.

Chihuahua   Ears large and upright but set at an angle of forty five degrees with the forehead, in much the same way as the 'butterfly' ears of the Papillon, its probable relative.

Griffon
Bruxellois Small, semi-erect, set high on the head.

Greyhound Small, fine and rose-shaped, tending to lie back upon upper part of the neck.

Collie Ears small and rather wide at the base with plenty of space between them but must not lie too near the side of the head. While at rest carried back but on the alert they become erect at their bases with the tips of the ears drooping forwards.

Alsatian Ears set high, wide at base, rather large and pointed but not over large nor too small. Erect and tilted slightly forwards.

Dobermann Small, neat and set high on head, triangular in shape. They may droop forward close to the cheek, or they may be erect, which is preferred.

Kerry Blue Small, triangular and drooping close over the cheeks.

Lakeland
Terrier Ears small to medium, triangular and not set quite so high on the head.

Yorkshire
Terrier Ears small, triangular and set rather high generally, carried erect.

Great Dane Ears medium in size, set rather high, and pendant.

Pomeranian Small and erect, tending to point forwards. Comparatively wide at the base.

Samoyed Ears triangular and erect, with short coat covering them. Inclined to face a little outwards.

Schipperke Medium in length, fairly broad at the base, erect, firm and opening usually facing forwards.

Welsh Corgi Owing to the convex skull the ears appear to be
(Cardigan) set rather widely apart. Wide at the base, fully erect and pointed at the tips.

Welsh Corgi Skull wide between the ears with well filled-out
(Pembroke) cheeks and only slight stop. Ears wide at base, tapering to rounded tips, erect and facing fully forward.

Elkhound Ears triangular, set high on the head, wide at base,

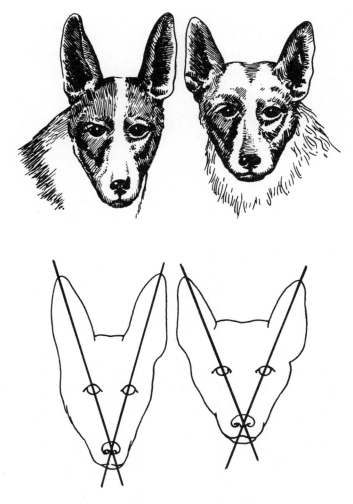

Fig. 14   Welsh Corgi   Welsh Corgi
(Cardigan)   (Pembroke)

In the Cardigan the ears are longer and larger with less space between them on top of the head.
In each dog a line drawn from the top of the ear to the centre of the nose passes through the eye.

	tapering sharply to a point, and leaning forward.
Chow Chow	Ears small, triangular and erect, tilted slightly forwards.
Pug	Ears small and thin and may be either 'button', or 'rose'. Button ears are preferred.
French Bulldog	'Bat' ears of medium size, erect. Wide at the base, rounded at the tops and looking well forward.

THE EYES

Many puppies as soon as their eyelids open, appear to have milky white or blue eyes but provided the eyes are perfect in size and shape these usually darken quite rapidly.

In the majority of breeds a dark eye is required, or in other words a deeply pigmented iris. Quite frequently the iris is not deeply pigmented, with a fully pigmented rim surrounding the pupil and this may cause the eye to appear better in some lights than in others, as the pupil closes to a pinpoint in bright sunlight but opens widely in the dull light often attendant upon indoor exhibitions.

To a certain extent eye colour may be linked with coat colour so that a Yellow Labrador with a hazel eye is less conspicuous than a black Cocker with a light eye. Fortunately, the latter is not commonly met with. The Golden Retriever should have dark eyes.

In the Clumber Spaniel the eyes are carried well back in the orbits and are dark amber in colour. In the Cocker they are similar although really dark eyes are preferred, but in Springers a hazel or dark brown eye is accepted, in accordance with the general body colour.

In the brachycephalic breeds the eyes are usually more prominent than in the long-headed breeds and most of them possess really dark or black eyes, apart from some of the lighter-coloured Pekingese which may have paler eyes; not popular with judges.

Some breeds, especially Chow Chows, are particularly subject to turning-in of the eyelids (Entropion). Until recently these could not be operated on and subsequently shown but this rule has now been waived partly on grounds of humanity.

If we recapitulate part of the foregoing remarks, we may

inquire why some breeds retain certain points or features? The answer must surely be that such breeds developed characteristics which fitted them for the particular work they were bred to perform.

For example, we remarked that greyhounds required particularly long necks but there was no comment derived from the breed Standard regarding the width of the nasal bones.

This is because the greyhounds, or to make the matter more comprehensive, the Gazehounds, which include all the breeds which hunt by sight, hunt without putting into operation their sense of smell.

This may be sound in theory but in actual fact it is not completely true. I have frequently watched an old greyhound whose sight was rapidly failing, track a rabbit across a field at dusk, using its nose as well as any Beagle could have done. But this is all by the way.

What a half-blind greyhound might do is no indication as to what that same dog may have done in its heyday. It merely shows that when unable to employ one of its senses, it was quite able to fall back upon another. When it possesses both the sense of sight and that of smell, it preferred the former.

Another reason why the greyhound should have a long neck is not related to eyes or vision but to the belief that those with shorter necks lack speed. The Standard of the Foxhound, a breed which hunts almost entirely by scent, refers to this theory by associating a short neck with lack of pace.

Could it be that the greater effort to get the nose to the ground required when the neck is short, handicaps the fore limbs in their attempts to take long strides?

If this be the reason it would not apply to greyhounds which have no occasion to get head to ground other than when attempting to 'pick' their game.

What does a Gazehound require in the matter of eyesight?

In the first place it is essential for it to be able to see an object a great distance ahead. A short-sighted greyhound would not be of any great use at work. It must be able to see a moving object a hundred yards away if the ground is clear.

Years ago the Cornish farm lads used to catch their rabbits

at night by the process of 'lamping'. Cornwall was then the original home of the Greyhound. Trained dogs would see a rabbit in a white, moving spot in the small area lit by the pencil-like beam of the torch, usually run off a car battery.

It would be interesting to know whether a gazehound is able to employ binocular vision, i.e. see an object with two eyes simultaneously; to be precise, can it see a rabbit at a considerable distance with both eyes at once?

In the majority of long-headed dogs such as the Greyhound the two eyes are set a little obliquely towards the side of the head. The usual angle of divergence from the centre line of the head is approximately 30 degrees. One eye, therefore, looks away to the right and the other to the left and the only way to keep a rabbit directly in front in view is to keep the head moving on the end of a long neck and catch glimpses of it with one eye at a time.

In some of the short-faced breeds, the Pugs and the Pekingese, the eyes are not set obliquely but frontally like our own, and in these breeds binocular vision is easier. The dogs can see an object directly in front of the head using both eyes simultaneously.

They can therefore decide on its shape and can focus upon it.

There is one breed, not a member of the brachycephalic (short-faced) breeds which is gradually becoming able to see ahead with both eyes at once, since its eyes which were once set at 30 degrees like those of the greyhound are now becoming frontally placed like our own, or like those of the Pekingese. This is the Poodle, and the transformation at present is more obvious in the Toys, then in the miniatures and least in the Standards, in which a fraction of the upper end of the nasal bones still tends to separate the eyes as it must have done in the original Standard Poodles.

Let us now refer to the Standards of some of the Gazehounds and note how the breed clubs refer to them:

Greyhound   Eyes bright and intelligent, dark in colour.
Whippet   Eyes bright, expression very alert.
Saluki   Dark to hazel and bright, but not prominent.
Borzoi   Eyes dark, intelligent and alert. Almond-shaped,

set obliquely, placed well back but not too far apart. Eye rims dark. Eye should not be light, round or staring.

In a group in which the eye is so important a factor and in view of the fact that we are endeavouring to maintain the elements of working ability, it seems surprising that no attempt has been made to increase the degree of frontality in eye placement, something after the style in which it is now developing in the Poodle.

The colour of the eye or of the eye rims, has no effect on vision so one may wonder whether those who first drew up the Standards thought that a dark eye was superior in vision to a light eye, or if, after all, the whole subject of the Standard was to make each breed in its own way, pretty.

The respective Standards make no reference to the fact that certain breeds have flat faces, frontal eye placement and binocular vision while others have long heads with prominent muzzles separating the two eyes, each of which has its own separate field of vision.

Probably the reason is that there is apparently no co-operation or means of communication between the people who drew up the Standards in differing breeds.

Compare the Standards regarding the eyes in two entirely different breeds.

Pug

Eyes dark in colour, very large, bold and prominent, globular in shape, soft and solicitous in expression, very lustrous when excited full of fire.

Dandie Dinmont

Eyes set wide apart, large, round but not protruding, bright, expressive of great determination, intelligence and dignity, set low and prominent in front of the head; colour, a rich hazel.

The point I am trying to make is that one could exchange these two descriptions, apart perhaps from actual colour. The first dog is flat-faced with its eyes placed frontally like our own, able to use both eyes simultaneously.

The second dog is a long-headed dog with a strong skull, broad between the eyes having a forehead well domed, which

completely separates the eyes so that vision must be mono-
cular; in other words these eyes can probably only see a
distant object, singly.

I am not suggesting that either Standard is in any way wrong
in its actual description of the eyes in either breed. Only that
they are set in two entirely different types of head, *of which no
mention is made*. The fact that one of the dogs has frontal eye
placement like our own and can see as we do, and that the
other has not and cannot, seems to me to be worth recording
in at least one of the Standards.

About the only recognition of frontal eye placement is to be
found in the following Standard.

Yorkshire Terrier

Eyes, medium, dark and sparkling, having a sharp, intelligent expression and placed so as to look directly forward. They
should not be prominent and the edges of the eyelids should be
of a dark colour.

An eye of some interest is encountered in the *Japanese Spaniel*:
Eyes should be large, dark, set well apart. It is desirable that the
white shows in the inner corners that gives the Japanese that
characteristic look of astonishment (wrongly called 'squint'),
which should on no account be lost.

One of the most detailed descriptions concerns the eye of the
Bloodhound. The eyes are deeply sunk in the orbits, the lids
assuming a lozenge or diamond shape in consequence of the
lower lid being dragged down and everted by the heavy flews.

The eyes correspond with the general colour of the animal,
varying from deep hazel to yellow. The hazel colour is to be
preferred although very seldom seen in liver and tan (red and
tan) hounds. The eye should be free of interference from the
eyelashes.

Another very detailed description relates to the eyes of the
Bulldog. The eyes seen from the front should be situated low
down in the skull, as far from the ears as possible. The eyes
and 'stop' should be in the same straight line which should be
at right angles to the furrow. They should be as wide apart as
possible, provided their outer quarters are within the outline
of the cheeks. They should be quite round in shape, of

moderate size, neither sunken nor prominent, and in colour should be very dark, almost if not quite black, showing no white when looking forward.

In the Terriers as a whole, the eye is seldom prominent, appearing small and sunken with what the old-timers termed 'a varminty expression'.

The eyes of the Bedlington are described as being triangular. This applies also to those of the Bull Terrier.

In the Staffordshire Bull Terrier the eyes are dark and may be related to coat colour. They are round, of medium size, set to look straight ahead.

In the Mastiff the eyes are small, wide apart, divided by at least the space of two eyes, the darker the better.

The Weimeraner has eyes of light amber, or hazel.

In the Welsh Corgi (Pembroke) the eyes are well set, round, medium size, hazel in colouring and blending with colour of coat.

In this breed a line drawn from the tip of the nose through the eye should, if extended, pass through, or close to, the tip of the ear.

In the following breeds some variation from the more common dark eye appears in their respective Standards.

Weimeraner

Light amber or hazel, but when dilated under excitement such eyes should appear nearly black.

Collies

These have a dark eye but in merles the eyes may be blue-white or china.

Old English Sheepdog

Dark eyes or wall eyes.

Welsh Corgis

Dark eyes, but silver eyes are permissible in Blue merles.

Bedlington Terriers

Blue and tans may have lighter eyes with silver lights.

Afghan

Dark eyes but golden colour not debarred.

Bloodhound

Deep hazel to yellow. Especially in red and tan hounds.

Dachshunds

Dapples or Chocolates may have wall or light eyes.

Big Eyes	Round Eyes	Almond Eyes	Small	Oval	Tri-angular
Bearded Collie	Welsh Corgi	Alsatian Boxer	Mastiff	Schnauzer	
Griffon	Boston Terrier	Bull mastiff	Newfound- land	Pomeranian	
	Bulldog	Dobermann	St. Bernard		
		Great Dane	Chow	Dachshund	
Italian Greyhound	Dalmatian	Pyrenean Mountain	Chow Schipperke	Saluki	
Japanese	French Bulldog	dog Samoyed	Min Pin		
		Shetland		Norfolk Terrier	
Cavalier King Charles	Shih Tzu Chihuahua	Sheepdog Chow		Manchester Terrier	
		Chow Keeshond			
	Griffon	Poodle			
		Setters			Afghan
		Pointers			
	Cavalier King Charles	Retrievers Spaniels (except			Bull Terrier
	Maltese	American			
	Papillon	Cocker)			
	Pekingese	Basenji			
	Pug	Basset Hound			
	American Cocker	Beagle Borzoi			
	Weimeraner	Deerhound			
	Rhodesian Ridgeback	Elkhound Finnish			
	Fox Terriers	Spitz Greyhound			
	Sealyham Terrier	Whippet Terriers			
	Staffordshire Bull Terrier	(not otherwise classified)			
	Welsh Terrier				

3

The neck and shoulders

It seems advisable to consider the neck and shoulders together, because they coalesce without apparent division — or should do so — and there is a very close association between neck and shoulders, metaphorically as well as physically.

One of the things that makes it difficult to breed and win, is the fact that in so many varieties the standard calls for a long neck and a short back, whereas the normal tendency is for all the spinal bones to be relatively long or relatively short.

Whatever the length of the neck, it still contains the regulation number of seven cervical bones so that in the exhibition specimen it is usually presumed that each of the seven will be longer than normal and each of the thirteen dorsal vertebrae will be shorter. An interesting point for the genetecists!

Within the neck the cervical bones start from immediately behind the cranium, pass along the lower portion of the neck above the trachea (or windpipe), then pass between the two scapulae (bladebones) and ascend to meet the first dorsal bone between these, and quite close to their upper borders.

It will be gathered from the above that the neck bones are curved within the neck with the concavity of the curve uppermost.

Every neck has two ends, one of which joins the cranium and the other articulates with the first dorsal bone. Both are equally important so far as the appearance of the dog is concerned.

The manner in which the upper end joins the skull, decides how the head is set on the neck and whether it is nicely

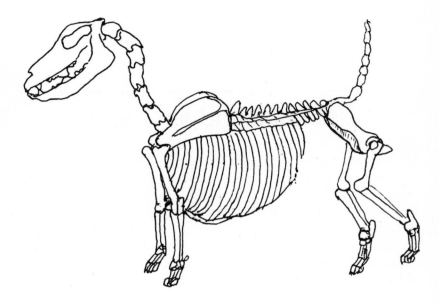

Fig. 15   Skeleton of Scotch Terrier

elevated, or if it is to be carried low and lacking distinction.

This depends more upon the portion of the articulation carried by the skull than upon that carried by the neck.

If we compare the skulls of a man and an Alsatian, we find that in man the medulla, which is continued as the spinal cord, emerges from the lower part of the skull, in order to enable him to stand upright and balance his head *above* the spine.

In the Alsatian, as in most other breeds, the neural canal, the foramen or aperture through which the medulla passes, is carried *behind* the skull close below the occiput.

In individual dogs there is a little variation as to the actual position of the neural canal and this contributes largely to the manner in which the head is carried.

In the short-faced or brachycephalic breeds the canal is usually carried rather lower, and this can be appreciated when comparing the head carriage of a Pekingese with that of an Alsatian.

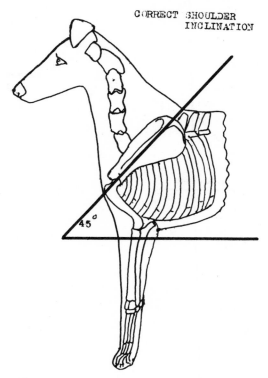

Fig. 16   Correct shoulder inclination

In the majority of cases a long neck goes in company with a sloping, well inclined scapula, in other words with a good shoulder; while a short neck more frequently accompanies an upright shoulder.

Whether the shoulder is to be well inclined — as it should be — or upright will depend considerably upon the length of the dorsal bones, or at any rate upon the length of the first eight of the thirteen, since the scapula is united to the spinal bones throughout the length of the first eight and unless these bones are sufficiently long, the scapula could not slope backwards at the required angle.

The dorsal bones give anchorage to the upper ends of the thirteen pairs of ribs and it follows that if the dorsal bones (as well as the cervical bones) have to be long, there is a danger

41

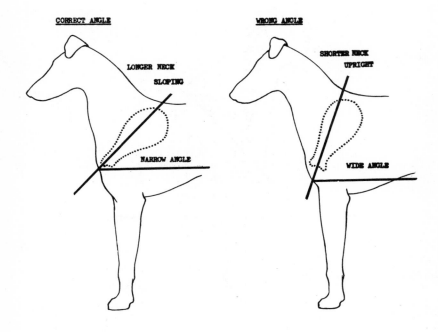

CORRECT ANGLE

WRONG ANGLE

LONGER NECK

SLOPING

NARROW ANGLE

SHORTER NECK

UPRIGHT

WIDE ANGLE

Fig. 17   Inclined and upright shoulders

that the back will also be long, which in most breeds would be regarded as a serious fault.

As it happens, however, a body that is 'well ribbed back' is admired.

The shortening has therefore to take place in the remainder of the spine, occupied by the seven lumbar bones, that is to say between the last rib and the sacrum. The answer, therefore, is that a dog requires long cervical bones, long dorsal bones, and short lumbar bones.

These limit the length of body between the last rib and the front of the dog's thigh, which is what is wanted in order that the dog may appear to be short-coupled, without being unduly slack behind the ribs. The last rib in the dog is a short 'floating' rib not attached at its lower end.

The whole difficulty, of course, is to obtain the short lumbar bones in connection with a lengthy neck and dorsal vertebrae.

Whether the shortening or lengthening of any part of the spine arises from variations in the thickness of the inter-vertebral cartilaginous discs, or of the bones, is a matter of little consequence to exhibitor or judge, but to the genetecist, it is of considerable interest.

Apart from the head and neck, the shoulder is one of the most important parts of the body so far as the show dog is concerned, not only on the score of beauty but also because a shoulder that is 'well laid back' makes it easier to advance the forelimbs, and is essential to graceful, easy and rapid pro-gression.

The portion of the body overlying the posterior angles of the two scapulae and the superior spinous processes of the seventh and eighth dorsal vertebrae is known as the *wither*.

In the dog the wither is not so well-developed nor as high as in the average horse but in certain breeds it is better developed than in others, with the result that the dog may then appear slightly higher at the wither than at the stern, so that the body appears to slope downwards from the base of the neck to the tail. In the Boxer the wither is high where it joins the neck, and although the Standard describes the back as broad and straight, at all times when the dog strains forward as in pulling on the lead, the body bends to slope markedly downwards from the wither to tail.

In the Dobermann and Pointer the back slopes downward slightly, while in the exhibition Greyhound the body is rather high at the wither and then slopes a little downward from sacrum to tail root.

The Standard of the American Cocker requires the body to slope evenly from the withers to the set-on of tail.

The neck must anastomose with the shoulders in all parts without any distinct line of demarcation except at the line running from shoulder joint to wither, where there will be a narrow, rather flattened surface where neck and shoulder meet.

This surface indicates the angle of inclination of the scapula.

In a well inclined shoulder this flattened surface will slope rapidly backward toward the wither.

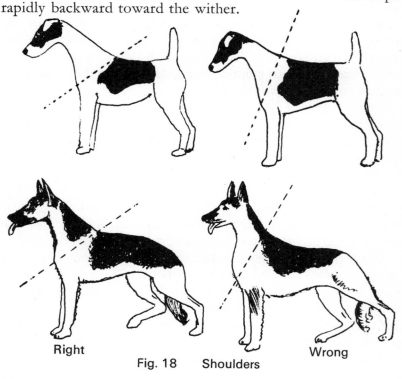

Right   Wrong

Fig. 18   Shoulders

In a bad, upright shoulder the shoulder joint itself (the point of the shoulder) will lie almost directly below the wither and the flattened, narrow surface where neck and shoulder meet on either side, will be almost perfectly upright. This is always a major fault.

The upper central line of the neck should slope gracefully over the wither so that there is no definite line or point of demarcation. In some cases the Breed Standards demand that the rear line of the neck shall be slightly arched. Good handlers leave as much hair as the case demands above the root of the neck. Removing it, even when profuse, is apt to leave a severe line of demarcation and completely ruin the continuity of neck and withers.

One should study the respective Breed Standards concerning the shape of the neck, and particularly as to its treatment as regards coat.

The neck must show muscle principally over the line of the neck bones. Some Standards want the neck flattened on the sides, others demand that the neck shall be rounded.

That applying to the Boston Terrier more nearly complies with the general demand:

'Of fair length, slightly arched and carrying the head gracefully; neatly set into the shoulders.'

On a few occasions a short neck is demanded, but in the Bulldog the Standard reads:

'Neck should be moderate in length (rather short than long), with much loose, thick and wrinkled skin about the throat, forming a dewlap on each side, from the lower jaw to the chest.'

As a contrast in the French Bulldog:

'The neck should be powerful, with loose skin at the throat, but not exaggerated. Well arched and thick, but not too short.'

In the Tibetan Apso and the Tibetan Spaniel:

'The neck is short and strong and well covered with a mane, more pronounced in dogs than in bitches.'

45

In the Schipperke:

'The neck is strong and full, rather short set, broad on the shoulders and slightly arched.'

The Standard also asks for shoulders muscular and sloping in this breed, a combination not easy to encounter in company with the sort of neck demanded.

In the Pomeranian, 'The neck is rather short and well set in.'

In the Terriers, Hounds and Gundogs the general demand is for a moderately long neck.

In the Gazehounds a *long* neck is required.

Probably the best way to determine whether the shoulder is upright or inclined gracefully is to locate the upper end of the spine of the scapula and hold a finger of the right hand on this point while a finger of the left hand rests on the point of the shoulder. A real or imaginary line may be drawn to connect these two points.

The line if continued to the table on which the dog stands, would meet it at approximately 45 degrees, while the angle between the lower end of the scapula and the humerus should be approximate 90 degrees.

There is another part of the shoulder which may require examination.

This is at the wither where the upper ends of the two scapulae, lie close beneath the skin. With the head level one should be able to insert the tips of one or two fingers between these.

While the finger is in position, lower the dog's head and' note the nutcracker effect upon the fingertip.

In order to have fine shoulders the Standard of the Exhibition Greyhound states that the shoulders should be narrow and cleanly defined at the top. But unless two fingers can be inserted, a tall Greyhound cannot get its head to the ground at full speed to pick up a hare or rabbit. It can only feed from a dish on the ground by kneeling or throwing the legs apart.

This same remark applies to some of the exhibition Fox Terriers, so fine at the upper ends of the shoulders that they cannot kill a quickly moving rat.

However, the Standard calls for this conformation and judges must conform with the Standard, until or unless it is changed.

4

The fore-end of the dog

It is well to point out at this stage of the work that the shoulders, arms and forelimbs are not attached to the body by any bony union, articular or otherwise.

The *thorax*, made up from the ribs, forming an enclosure termed 'the rib cage', is slung, like a cradle, between two upright posts.

These posts are represented in the body of the dog by the forelimbs, containing the scapula, humerus, radius and ulna, knee bones, phalanges and feet, in this order. The rib cage is attached to the limbs by means of muscles. These comprise muscles beneath the scapula, passing from the scapula to the cervical and dorsal vertebrae and to the ribs themselves.

These muscles are soft structures, capable of contraction and expansion. It becomes obvious, therefore, that the rib cage within the upright limb bones is capable of a considerable degree of movement.

The outcome of this is that the body can actually change its position between the limbs at will. It does this more probably in the horse than in the dog because the horse has a body, comparatively rigid with little or no spinal flexion outside the very movable neck. The body of the dog is highly flexible in almost any direction.

However, even in the dog, the freedom of the thorax (rib cage) within its upright supports is taken advantage of during galloping, jumping and even on occasion during walking, particularly on a slippery surface. Owing to its presence the body moves with much more freedom than it could without this arrangement.

. Corwick Amber of Little Breach.
ner: Mrs. L. R. Percival

KING CHARLES SPANIEL
Ch. Huntglen Black Narcissus.
Owner: Mrs. Madeline Harper.

IFFON
Gaystock le Nouveau.
ner: Mrs. D. Gaines.

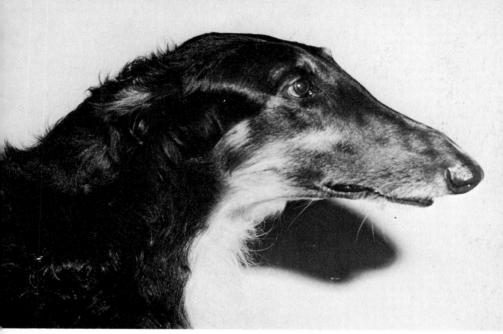

Ch. Black Diamond of Enolan.

Ch. Black Tarquin of Enolan.

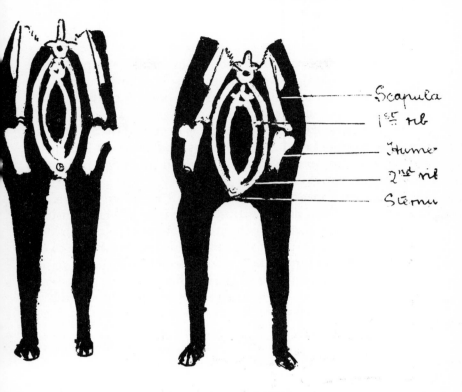

Fig. 19   Section of Thorax
Showing how the thorax is cradled between the scapulae.

In the horse one sees the mechanism at work to the greatest advantage among the 'cutting ponies' of Australia but in dogs it is especially useful among racing Greyhounds tackling a bend in the track, and during coursing.

Naturally, it functions most in tall dogs such as Greyhounds, the Gazehounds generally, and in Great Danes and the larger varieties of gundog.

It is now easier to see why I speak of 'the fore-end' of the dog because the head, neck, shoulders and fore-limbs, plus the portion of the thorax suspended between them, constitute a separate unit.

49

The hindlimbs with the lumbar portion of the spine and abdomen together constitute what one may term the 'hinder-end'.

The portion between these, containing the greater part of the spine, the diaphragm with the thorax in front of it, and the abdomen behind it, constitute the mid-portion of the body.

Let us now return to the fore-end.

The space between the forelimbs is occupied by the anterior end of the thorax containing lungs and heart and enclosed within the first four pairs of ribs which lie between the two scapulae, or shoulderblades.

What may appear to be a very small item — the degree of curvature of these first few ribs, is a matter of very considerable importance from the exhibition viewpoint. Not only does the degree of curvature of the ribs decide the distance between the forelimbs but it makes a considerable difference to the front action, the handling of the forelimbs.

The two scapulae are held together at their upper ends by means of the muscles which unite them to the dorsal spine as well as to the ribs.

If the curvature of the first four ribs is excessive then the elbows will be somewhat handicapped in their freedom of movement, the elbows will be thrust apart and the front action will be greatly impaired.

The ideal ribs are those in which the first few pairs are almost straight, but following these each pair of ribs should become a little more curved than the preceding pair especially at their upper ends, up to the eleventh or twelfth pairs. The thirteenth pair are the so-called floating ribs, unattached at their lower extremities.

In addition to throwing out the elbows, excessive curvature of the first four or five pairs of ribs, will throw the shoulder joints outward and even a small degree of this will give rise to 'pintoeing', and in a terrier, will completely spoil the 'straight front'.

The difficulty in producing a show dog is enhanced by the fact that in most breeds we must have long neckbones, long dorsal bones, short lumbar bones and ribs which are abnor-

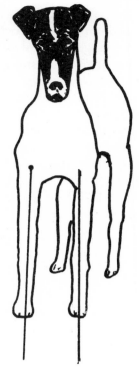

Fig. 20   Terrier Front
A little wide between arms owing to too marked curvature of front ribs.

mally straight at the front and abnormally curved at the rear end.

Then we get minor problems in the way of slack elbows, curvature of limb bones, slack pasterns, and feet which turn in when they ought to turn out, or vice versa, and when we have got everything we want in body shape, we find we have a dog that refuses to show. This is looking at the black side, but even in dog breeding and showing, it is not always Friday the thirteenth, and on the whole the chances of making-up a champion are a little greater than that of winning a football pool, so take heart.

Since ribs play such a definite part in shaping the fore-end, we may as well consider them more generally.

As well as having a variable degree of curvature, ribs have length. Additional length produces a deeper chest which in many instances is an advantage. But only so far as the degree of curvature and the length of rib correspond both in degree and in the position of the greater curvature.

A shortish rib, well curved throughout its length produces a round barrel chest. If the ribs are also long enough and you are breeding Bulldogs your luck is in, but if your favourites are Smooth Fox Terriers you will not be so lucky since the Standard insists that the chest shall not be broad and neither shall it be excessively deep since while too narrow a chest is almost as undesirable as a broad one, excessive depth of brisket and chest is an impediment to a Terrier when going to ground.

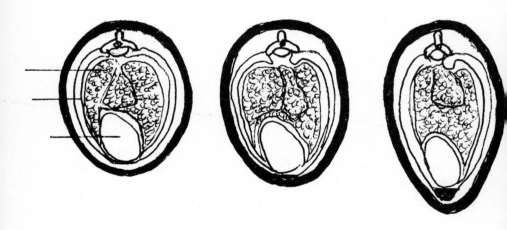

Fig. 21   Types of chest shapes in section

Ribs in most dogs, particularly working terriers, should be rather straight in the first few but should become wider as they travel backwards and it is to be hoped that the dorsal vertebrae are long and the lumbar bones very short so that the Terrier is well ribbed back and very short in the couplings, the space between the last rib and the stifle.

Chests have altered a lot in shape during the past thirty years as the result of selective breeding. The original chest was usually wide without a great deal of depth, the 'barrel-chest' of the primitive wolf, which, by the way, was no mean performer in a long chase. Probably the cubic capacity of the barrel chest was greater than that in a Fox Terrier, let us say thirty or forty years ago than it is today, but the present chest looks nicer and is more pleasing to the artistic eye.

The writer can remember that the older type of Terrier, the Jack Russell, many of which came into his family possession when the Parson died, carried barrel chests and were not particularly low on the leg as people nowadays imagine. They certainly were not always quite as large as the modern 'Wire', but they had no difficulty in going to ground. Their main difficulty seemed to be getting back again and it seemed that a large portion of the writer's juvenile life was spent with pick and shovel.

They (the old Jack Russells) had one characteristic, a fairly straight stifle and hock which did not impede them in a narrow run. It is unlikely that the longer tibia and well-bent hock of the modern terrier would serve as well.

A breed which has not been 'improved' so far as shape of chest and chest capacity is concerned is the *Staffordshire Bull Terrier*. This is not a breed required to move very rapidly and for the purposes for which the breed was originally employed a modern chest would not be advantageous, nor is it likely that a dog of this breed would be any more happy if it could claim to have been 'made' more pretty than Nature ordained. Any attempt to lengthen the ribs would have necessitated lengthening the forelimbs.

One of the faults most common in the bigger breeds so far as chest development is concerned is not so much in the depth of the ribs as in their curvature.

In the *Pyrenean* a flat chest with considerable depth is demanded but in a *Great Dane* one must have the rib curvature as well.

In the *Shetland Sheepdogs* the chest must be deep and wide at the top part but must taper down as the ribs descend to make additional room for free arm movement.

The *Alsatian* must not be slab-sided but too much rib curvature constitutes a fault. Nevertheless when compared

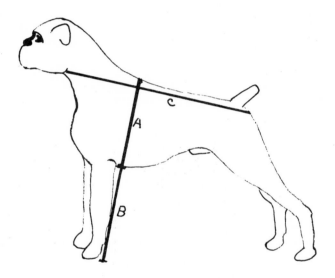

Fig. 22   In the Boxer A = B and A + B = C

with many breeds of similar size the ribs of the Alsatian might be considered as 'rather flat'.

The *Irish Setter* is an example of a breed requiring a deep, well sprung chest only at its hinder end. The anterior ribs should preferably be much straighter. This is also the type of chest required in the *German Short Haired Pointer*, while in the *English Pointer* the chest should not be over wide in front.

In the *Irish Water Spaniel* the ribs must be well-sprung behind the shoulders so as to give a barrel-like appearance to the body but with normal width and curvature of the first few ribs between the shoulder blades. The ribs must be carried far back.

In the *Sussex Spaniel* a rather similar requirement is made, the body being barrel-shaped from behind the elbows and carried back.

In the *Bull Terrier* the body should be rounded with good spring of rib, and great depth from withers to brisket so that the latter is nearer the ground than the belly, which should form a graceful upward curve. Viewed from the front of the dog the chest should look very wide.

In none of the smaller terriers, the *Lakeland*, the *Welsh* or the *West Highland* should the ribs be too curved, particularly near the front of the chest.

Hounds generally, that hunt, should not be ribbed too far back, in other words they should not be so short coupled as Terriers as they gallop better when they have a little room between ribs and stifles.

This does not apply so much to the *Basset Hound* which normally has enough slack in the flanks to permit the ribs to be curved from behind the shoulder, back to the flanks.

The *Dachshund* which does little or no galloping is ribbed right back to the flanks.

In the *Ibizan Hound* (Pudenco) the ribs are rather flat and hardly reach down to the elbow. They are, however, carried very far back.

The *Italian Greyhound* requires a chest deep, but narrow.

The *Pomeranian* must be well ribbed-up and the barrel well rounded.

The *Bedlington Terrier* is flat-ribbed but deep through the brisket. It must be well ribbed back.

In the *Boxer,* the chest should be deep and reach down to the elbows. The ribs should be well-arched but not barrel-shaped. They should extend well to the rear, remembering that the belly rises gracefully from the Xiphoid cartilage at the rear end of the sternum until level with the stifle.

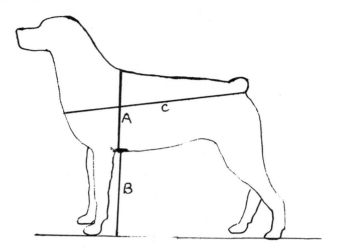

Fig. 23   In the Rottweiler A = B and A + B = C

The depth of the Boxer's chest should measure from withers to sternum, the same as from the sternum to the ground.

In the *Bulldog* the chest is very wide and laterally round, prominent and deep, making the dog appear very broad and short-legged in front. The ribbing must extend well back to the flank.

In the little *Border Terrier* the body is deep and narrow and fairly long. The ribs are carried well back but not oversprung as the terrier should be *capable of being spanned by both hands behind the shoulder.*

In the *German Short Haired Pointer* the chest is deep rather than wide. It should be considerably less well sprung for a handsbreadth behind the elbow to allow free play for the shoulders and forearm.

THE FORELIMBS

Anatomy

The shoulder and scapula and humerus have already been discussed. It might be well to mention again the fact that certain Standards, notably those of the Greyhound and Whippet require little space between the upper ends of the scapula. This, carried to excess, prevents the dog getting its nose to the ground. There is in some quarters a tendency to a similar

conformation in the Fox Terriers, although this is not specific-
ally called for in their Standards. A terrier with the two
scapulae almost in contact at their upper surfaces would have
difficulty in reaching a rat on the ground.

The Elbow

This joint is attached to the thorax by the pectoral muscles
on either side of the body.

The pectoral muscles run under the breast. They are attached
at one end to the sternum and at the other end to the inner
side of the shoulder joint. These muscles play a considerable
part in forelimb movement, not an active part, as they do not
bring the limb forward or backward, but they support the
elbows and permit them to approach, rest upon, or draw away
from, the side of the chest.

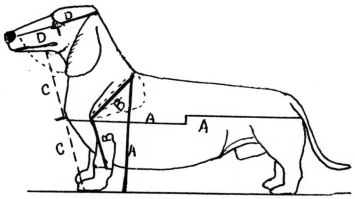

Fig. 24   Some Dachshund measurements
All lines bearing the same letter are of equal length.

If they are weakly or not functioning well, the elbows appear
loose and sloppy. They may then permit the legs to wobble
and the feet to turn in (pintoeing), or outwards, when the
dog walks.

The *Elbow joint* is made up from the lower articular surface
of the humerus and the upper end of the radius and ulna. The
upper end of the ulna is drawn out into a solid projection, the
olecranon process, which stands upright behind the elbow
joint. Corresponding with this at the lower, hind end of the
humerus is a cavity in the bone which receives the olecranon

process when the dog is standing with weight on the foot. The fit is so good that when the dog stands squarely with weight on BOTH fore feet, neither fore leg can be moved forward (as in starting off) until a hind limb has taken the weight off the front end of the body. The hind limb may do this either by flexing one hock and letting the weight fall on the tail end of the body; or alternatively, the dog may advance one hind foot under the belly and place weight on this, while it frees the arm to move the leg forward.

Both the radius and ulna in the dog are long bones. Both extend to the carpus or knee joint, and both articulate with knee bones, although at the lower end, above the knee, the radius provides the greater part of the articular surface.

The radius and ulna in most breeds (not in the Basset Hound, Tibetan Spaniel or Pekingese) need to be absolutely straight in order to maintain what is known as a 'good front'. Even the Bulldog with all its curves, must have a straight radius and ulna and not appear bowlegged, as it does in many pictures of the breed.

A 'straight front' as seen in most of the Terriers is not hard to recognise. As the eye travels down the dog which is standing facing you, you will note the front of the chest, whether it is normal or if it is abnormally broad between the points of the two shoulders. See Fig. 20.

You will then note how the two forelimbs emerge from the breast at elbow level, whether they are close together, medium, or too wide apart.

In a Fox Terrier the limbs will be placed well forward directly below the points of the shoulders. In a Cocker Spaniel the elbows would lie a little farther back under the chest and in each breed there is an optimum positioning for the elbows from which the fore legs descend.

In the Fox Terrier the forehand resembles that of a show hunter, as much as possible in front of the withers and the legs set well forward, the dog standing more on its toes than on its heel pads.

In a Fox Terrier, to quote as an example of what should be apparent in most breeds, a line dropped perpendicularly from

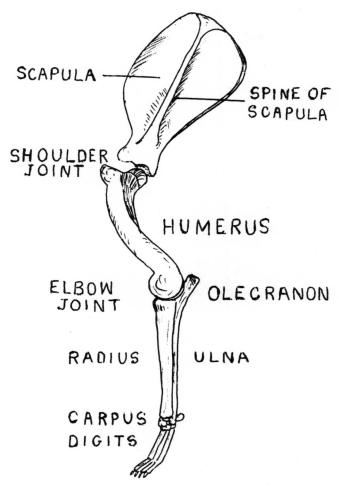

SCAPULA

SPINE OF SCAPULA

SHOULDER JOINT

HUMERUS

ELBOW JOINT

OLECRANON

RADIUS

ULNA

CARPUS
DIGITS

Fig. 25   Forelimb of a Corgi

the centre of the front of each elbow would travel down the centre line of the forearm, through the centre of the knee, down the pastern to pass between the second and third toes of the fore feet. See Fig. 20

The forearm needs to be thick and muscular, just as much so as the gaskin, or second thigh, in the hind limb. Both these limb portions take a big part in propelling the body and maintaining its weight, especially on such occasions as jumping down from a wall.

Considering how complicated a joint the knee is with its six flat bones and the seventh, the pisiform, acting as a lever at the rear of the joint, one rarely sees much trouble in it, but, nevertheless, the least fault in the position of any one of the bones will gravely effect the limb below it. Here we have the phalanges, four going to join the toes and one to the dew claw inside the limb.

The bones of the pastern and feet are controlled by a large assortment of muscles and ligaments.

Fig. 26
Some Basset Hounds have peculiar fronts but they usually pass so long as the knees do not knock together and the limbs can be fully extended in action.

Pasterns and Feet

These are very often the deciding factors in placing three very close-up dogs in their final order of merit. In nearly all breeds with the exception of some of the running breeds which use hair on the feet for the purpose of braking, and as a non-skid device, the feet need to be smooth, with well-defined toes neatly bunched together. Incidentally, whether the feet assume this closely-bunched style or remain flat with toes sprawling, depends on breeding and upon the pads which lie beneath the feet. Unless these, and particularly the central heart-shaped pad, are thick and well-formed in order to lift the foot, the feet will be slack or splayed.

Slack feet are usually accompanied by slack pasterns and a frequent contributor to flatness of feet is overgrowth of the toenails.

It is becoming fashionable to clip the nails, fore and hind, back close to their roots, at the same time that the dew claws, and tails are cut, in all cases in which this procedure is necessary. It is possible that docking of dogs may sooner or later become a thing of the past. Nevertheless, it is not kind to leave dew claws in position as they so often become broken and painful, or they may grow round and burrow deeply into the leg. In some breeds dewclaws must be present.

Nor, in breeds which work in rough cover, is it kind to leave a long tail.

The hind double dew claws of the Pyrenean almost invariably grow round into the limbs and penetrate the skin, producing painful septic wounds. Such are the dictates of Fashion.

Harking back to the subject of slack pasterns, there is only one treatment for these and that is to exercise the dog regularly, at walking pace on a surface which causes it to bunch its toes closely together.

This can be a *hard* surface, or a shaly one with imperfect foothold and small particles of stone which are liable to get between the toes if they are allowed to slacken. The dog should never be exercised on a smooth grass surface or even on smooth cement, which is very bad for feet and pasterns unless it is lightly strewn at all times with granite chippings, or small pebbles.

Dogs should not be asked to trot on this but only walk, otherwise they will damage their feet.

In isolated, rural districts, if any still exist, slow exercise behind a bicycle on the hardest of roads is still the ideal form of exercise.

Sheepdogs, high up on hillside farms, do not have slack pasterns since the hillsides are crumbly and grass is scarce. But, lower down where the cattle-dogs guard the cows, on comparatively flat grassland, bad feet and slack pasterns are quite commonly seen.

One of the greatest difficulties associated with exercising dogs in order to keep weight down and improve their feet, is that the average exhibitor, perhaps a little on the wrong side of middle age, is quite unable physically to walk the number of miles in a day required to bring a dog into show condition.

Some Forelimb Unsoundness

When viewed from either the front or the side, the forelimbs of most breeds (with the few exceptions previously noted) should be absolutely straight the whole way down to the feet.

In puppies, the curvature, when present, may arise from rickets. This may result from feeding foods deficient in vitamins A and D, or from a deficiency of calcium. There may be plenty of calcium present in the food but it may not be absorbed unless vitamin D is also present. In many cases rickets may result from excess of calcium, or lack of phosphorus in the food which is equally necessary.

Even when rickets is controlled by correcting the feeding, gently exercising in sunshine or with the help of ultra-violet lamps, does not correct the curvature and so the dog is useless for show.

Such bones may sometimes be straightened by operation but dogs thus treated are still unshowable and not good to breed from. A tendency to rickets may be hereditary.

'Out at elbows' — the elbows drifting away from the sides of the body — may be due to faulty muscular control from the pectoral muscles. As soon as this occurs and the elbows turn outwards the toes turn in.

Another cause of 'out-at-elbows' is a slight defect or distortion in the grooves on the lower end of the humerus where it articulates with the radius and ulna. This is also frequently the cause of pintoeing. The effects are particularly noticeable if the showring has a polished floor as it may do in a hall used at times for dancing. Dogs show this defect very readily when conditions make it necessary to 'put on the brakes'. Turning the toes inward is one of the easiest ways of avoiding slipping and skidding and brainy dogs soon pick up the habit and put it into action at the most difficult moments.

Pintoeing in less frequent cases results entirely from a hereditary fault in the elbow joint which cannot be remedied.

A common contributory factor to forelimb unsoundness is the habit of puppies jumping up and placing their fore feet on the outer door of their run or on the kennel doorway when locked from the outside.

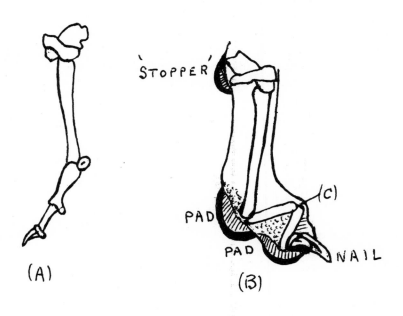

(A)

STOPPER

PAD

PAD

(C)

NAIL

(B)

Fig. 27   Bones of the Feet

In puppies up to twelve months or even older the ends of the long bones (epiphyses), the parts which carry the articular surfaces of the joints, are soft and cartilaginous, especially where they make contact with the main shaft of the bone.

Constantly jumping up at the inside of a closed door, moves these epiphyses a little upon the end of the long bone. The result is that when the cartilaginous union becomes permanent, the articular part may become welded solidly onto the shaft, still a little out-of-position.

It is possible in a puppy up to ten months to be mistaken into fancying that the limb bones are lumpy or out-of the-straight. The reason may be that the articulations in young dogs, especially in large dogs like Alsatians and Great Danes, are naturally much larger in comparison with the shafts of the limb bones than they will be when growth is complete.

At about 12-14 months the disparity in the sizes of joints and bones should disappear.

A dog may own a perfectly sound, straight front until one comes down to the toes, and these may be turned in or out or the dog may walk on its heels with the toe turned up, or turned under in front.

The feet themselves may not be of the type specified in the standard of the particular breed.

Normal Feet

Cat feet, must have the toes bunched together, resembling the foot of a cat.

Hare feet have the last or both pairs of digits within the foot, remaining slack, so that the whole foot is longer and flattened.

They often carry some long hair on top or between the toes, for braking purposes.

In the following breeds, the feet differ in some way from the normal bunched-up cat feet:

Afghan

Forefeet strong and very large in length and breadth, covered with long thick hair, toes arched. Hindfeet long but not so broad as front feet, covered with long thick hair.

Basset Hound

Feet massive, well-knuckled and padded. Feet may point

forward or slightly inward. All pads, centre and toes, to take equal shares of the weight.

Beagle

Front feet rather long, toes close together, well arched, never flat, neither turning in nor out. Hindfeet large, hare-like, larger and less arched.

Dachshund

Feet close and compact with well-arranged toes, nails strong.

Irish Wolfhound

Feet moderately large and round, turned neither inward nor outwards. Toes well arched and closed. Nails very strong and curved.

Rhodesian Ridgeback

Compact, well arched toes, with hair between them.

Saluki

Moderately long, toes long, not cat footed. Toes not splayed but well-feathered between.

Alsatian

Feet round, strong, slightly arched toes, held close together. Firm pads, strong short nails.

Bearded Collie

Oval, cat type with hair between toes.

Bullmastiff

Cat feet, splaying a decided fault.

Dobermann

Tight feet, cat like.

Pyrenean Mountain Dog

Feet close cupped. Double dew claw behind.

Samoyed

Long, flattish and slightly spread out. Soles well-cushioned with hair.

Gundogs

Feet well-arched and cat-like with well developed pads.

American Cocker

Hair between pads. Also between pads in Clumber spaniel, Field spaniel, Irish Water spaniel and Sussex spaniel.

Bedlington Terrier

Long hare feet with thick and well-closed up pads.

65

Cairn Terrier
Forefeet larger than hind and well closed-up pads. Feet may turn out slightly.

Dandie Dinmont
Flat feet objectionable. Feet of a pepper dog should be tan to pale fawn. In a mustard dog they are darker than its head. Hind feet much smaller than fore feet. Nails preferably black.

Manchester Terrier
Feet small. Semi-hare footed. Well arched toes.

West Highland White
Forefeet larger than the hind. All covered with short, hard hair. All nails and pads perfectly black.

French Bulldog
Feet continued in line of leg with absolutely sound pasterns. Hind feet rather larger than the front.

Shih Tzu
Feet firm and covered with a wealth.of hair.

Tibetan Spaniel
Hare footed, featherings between toes, white markings permitted.

Tibetan Terrier
Feet large, round, heavily furnished with hair between toes and pads.

Chihuahua
Small feet, neither hare nor cat feet. Fine pasterns, nails moderately long.

Black and Tan Old English Terrier
Jet black nails, well arched feet with two centre toes in front feet longer than the others. Hind feet cat type. Hare feet regarded as a fault.

Italian Greyhound
Long hare feet.

Japanese
Long hare feet.

Papillon
Fine and fairly long as in the hare. Large tufts of hair between toes.

Pekingese

Large and flat. Not round.

Pug

Neither quite hare feet nor quite cat feet.

THE TOP LINE

One sees constantly in judges' reports references to the 'top line'.

This varies a great deal in different breeds from the straight line (the straight line with a little extra muscle over the loins), to the Bedlington and the Italian Greyhound, where the body may be curved almost into a semicircle.

What happens to the line from croup to tail depends to some extent upon the natural degree of slope in each particular pelvis, and upon whether the sacrum is level, or raised a little at its hinder end. When the sacrum does lift behind one may expect the tail to be set on at a fairly high level, and vice versa.

In Terriers, the tail set-on of the docked tail is greatly influenced by the manner in which the sacrum lies as the tail bones are attached to it.

When the sacrum is dead level the Terrier will carry a good tail set at right angles to the spine.

Conversely when the sacrum dips slightly at its rear end the tail will also be inclined to be set on low so that it can be elevated to its normal height only with difficulty.

If the sacrum is elevated slightly at its rear end the tail will be carried gaily with a tendency for it to tilt forward over the back.

This does not apply to the 'broken' tail, the one which comes from a slightly down-tilted sacrum when the tail struggles in its lower half to become erect. It does this almost or completely so at its lower end but owing to some defect in the tail muscles the upper half tips forward or possibly backward. This is due mainly to abnormal pull of the tail muscles or a shortening of the muscles.

Many of these muscular contractions which keep tails bent and 'gay' as the judges term them, have a genetic background and follow certain familial lines.

Fig. 28   Showing the "top-line" in some of the running breeds.

Variations in the shape of the 'top line', welcome or otherwise as the case may be, depend upon similar variations in the height of the vertebral spines, usually those of the dorsal vertebrae or, maybe, those of the lumbar vertebrae. The height of the dorsal spines at about the fourth dorsal vertebrae will decide the height of the withers. In a Boxer, for example, a little additional height at the withers might be acceptable.

It would not be in a Whippet nor in a Cocker Spaniel but it might be acceptable in a Dobermann.

Further down the back, the spine may curve upwards and then again downwards, as in an Italian Greyhound.

In the Whippet from the withers half-way down the back is a straight line but after this the back curves a little upwards over the loins and then descends gently towards the tailhead. Part of the curvature over the loins is due to an increase in muscle but beneath this the spine also is curved.

In the Italian Greyhound the whole of the back from just behind the withers is curved constantly, as far back as the tailhead.

In our native Greyhound the degree of arching is slight and this is confined to the lumbar region, but as the loin and upper thigh of the greyhound are practically continuous the terminal part of the loin becomes almost as though it were a part of the hind limb when the greyhound gallops, with the hind feet actually passing the forefeet in their stride, while the loin and the thigh are both curved into almost a semicircle when the hind limb is stretched forward to its limit.

The dorsal vertebrae retain what is almost a straight line in the standing Greyhound and a degree of lumbar curvature in the standing Whippet but this is not the case in the Italian Greyhound in which the curvature is present in the dog during moments of relaxation as much as when excited and moving around a field.

In the remaining galloping breeds the back is less curved even than in the Whippet.

In the Afghan the back is level and of moderate length, well-muscled and falling away gently to the stern.

Fig. 29   More "top-lines"

In the Saluki, the back is fairly broad with muscles slightly arched over the loin.

In the Borzoi, the back rises in a graceful arch from as near the shoulder as possible, with a well balanced fall-away at the tail end. The degree of arching is greater in dogs than in bitches.

In the German Short Haired Pointer, the back is short and straight with a slight arching at the loins.

In this breed the loin and croup are wide and well covered with muscle.

Length of Back

In most of the gundogs the back is straight with a very slight rounding over the loins.

The tendency in many of the squarely built breeds is for the height from the wither to ground to approximately equal the length from the point of the shoulder to the seat bone.

In a few of the smaller breeds including some of the Toys, the body is relatively short.

The following tables show the relative heights of the body compared to the length.

In Column A the height and length of body are approximately equal.

In Column B the length slightly exceeds the height.

In Column C the length is definitely greater than the height.

In Column D the length is even greater.

A	B	C	D
Basenji	Afghan	Borzoi	Dachshund
Elkhound	Basset Hound	Deerhound	Dandie Dinmont
Saluki	Beagle	Irish Wolfhound	Skye Terrier
Whippet	Bulldog	Rhodesian	
Boxer	Finnish Spitz	Ridgeback	
Dobermann	Greyhound	Alsatian	
Airedale	Bearded Collie	Bullmastiff	
Border	Great Dane	Newfoundland	
Terrier	Old English	Australian	
Fox	Sheepdog	Terrier	
Terrier	Pyrenean	Scottish Terrier	
Lakeland	Mountain Dog	Retrievers	
Terrier	Rottweiler	Labradors	
Welsh	St. Bernard	Field Spaniel	
Terrier	Shetland	Sussex Spaniel	
Pomeranian	Sheepdog	Maltese	

71

A	B	C	D
American	Samoyed	Cavalier	
Cocker	Bedlington	Pembroke Corgi	
English	Terrier	Welsh Corgi	
Cocker	Bull Terrier		
Japanese	Cairn Terrier		
King Charles	Irish Terrier		
Kerry Blue	Norfolk Terrier		
Terrier	Springer Spaniel		
Manchester	Staffordshire		
Terrier	Bull Terrier		
Pug	W.H.W. Terrier		
Boxer	Pointer		
Schipperke	Chihuahua		
Dalmatian	Papillon		
Schnauzer	Pekingese		
Groenendael	Poodle		
	Chow Chow		
	French Bulldog		
	(or A)		
	Keeshond		
	Weimeraner		
	Sealyham Terrier		
	English Setter		
	Gordon Setter		
	Irish Setter		

5

The hindquarters

The pelvis of the dog is in a way comparable with the scapula in its effect upon the rest of the limb, as a result of the angle at which it lies in relation to the ground beneath it. We have already noted how the degree of inclination of the scapula affects the forelimb and the length of its stride. In perhaps a rather lesser degree the inclination of the pelvis influences the angulation of the hind limb and the length of its stride, although not quite so much as the scapula does in front, because the degree of variation of which the pelvis is capable is less.

There are two ways only in which the degree of inclination of the pelvis can be changed.

One is by moving forward or backward the fixed union between the ilium and the sacrum which is equivalent to moving forward or backward the sacrum itself. This can be done only by shortening or lengthening the lumbar vetebrae in front of the sacrum.

The other method would be to effect some change in the pelvis itself, whereby the acetabulum (which receives the head of the femur) would be nearer or farther from the tip of the ilium than it now is. Any of these changes could probably be effected within half a dozen generations by selective breeding scientifically carried out, probably with the help of X-ray.

But probably nothing good would come of it now since we are no longer dealing with the natural hind limb but with one which has already been scientifically deformed by lengthening the tibia, with the purpose of producing what is now known as 'angulation'.

The object has been to carry the point of propulsion, the part of the limb which makes contact with the ground, as far behind the body as possible. The purpose was to straighten the hind limb so that there was a direct drive from the ground, through the limb to the spine. But, unfortunately, those who organised this transformation had no regard for the acetabulum itself, the last station on the line between earth and spine.

The short straight limb that Nature provided directed the power upward as well as forward so that the drive into the acetabulum was diverted to its upper surface instead of to its anterior surface, as it is today.

Originally it *lifted* the pelvis and propelled the body forward, pelvis and all. Today it pushes upon the pelvis through the wrong portion within the acetabulum.

It would be useless to experiment further with this type of limb. If we wished to improve the original limb by selective breeding it might be possible to do so by improving the pelvis,

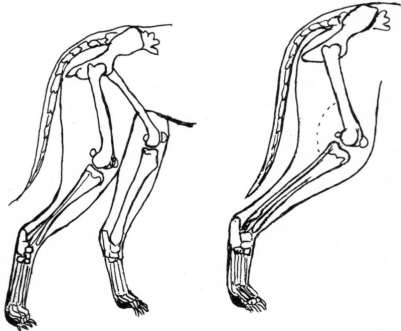

Fig. 30   Bones of the Hindquarters

not by lengthening the tibia. It is a little late in the day to contemplate this now as it would require entirely fresh stock to work with. The existing strains can never be improved, unless we go into reverse and lessen the degree of angulation rather than increase it.

As things are at present, judges, whether they like it or not, can only go by the Standards and place their awards as the Standards indicate.

One is apt to wonder sometimes when reading certain Standards carefully, whether they really *do* ask for the extremes which are now necessary if one is to win.

The Standard of the Greyhound, the dog with probably the longest tibia now, in any breed, reads:

'Loin powerful, slightly arched. Thighs and second thighs wide and muscular, showing great propelling power. Stifles well bent. Hocks well let down including neither inwards nor outwards. Body and hindquarters features should be of ample proportions and well coupled, enabling ample ground to be covered when standing.'

Personally, I can find no fault in this Standard. The fault is in its interpretation. The Greyhound has been exploited so that the present exhibition greyhound has difficulty in picking its game if it ever gets near enough to catch it, merely because its shoulder blades are so close together the dog cannot get its head down. It can no longer gallop as fast as it did fifty years ago. The little straight-stifled track dogs, nothing to look at from an exhibition angle, can run rings around the best show dogs, which with their present hind limbs could not get out of a trap anyway.

One Greyhound judge I discussed this with, more or less agreed that the modern show Greyhound was not of much use, but his argument was that we were breeding them not from the utility angle but purely for their beauty.

I don't know what the Cornish Greyhound breeders of fifty years ago would have replied to that, but I can hazard a pretty good guess.

The pelvis of the dog does not lie perpendicularly but at an angle approximately of 30-35 degrees with the horizontal.

It varies a little in shape in accordance with the breed as well as to a rather less extent in individuals. In the short legged, achondroplastic breeds such as the Scottish Terrier, the pelvis may be shortened in height more than in breadth. The orifice of the pelvis through which puppies have to pass before entering the world follows the general pattern so that the orifice instead of being oblong (higher than wide) becomes square, or even oblong from side to side which may make whelping quite difficult. As Scottie puppies also have quite large heads the difficulty becomes greater.

Bulldog breeders also decided that as their puppies have large round heads and fat bodies, it would make life more interesting if they decreed that the parents shall be pear-shaped with their hind ends smaller than the front. In consequence puppies' heads now find it difficult to emerge, so they dive below the pubis, the bone that bridges the floor of the pelvis, with the result that in frequent instances a Caesarian becomes necessary.

I mentioned previously that in the original dog the impulse of the foot pressing on the ground drove the round head of the femur up against the roof of the acetabulum and actually lifted the hind foot off the ground and pushed the body forward through space.

Now, if instead of lengthening the tibia and producing a marked angulation, we could have produced a dog in which the pelvis was tilted, ever so slightly more at the front end, a dog with even a short leg, or one nearly straight, would give the pelvis a *forward* impluse every time one hind foot pushed against the ground.

But this is all by the way. Until we see the light and start shortening the tibia again in quite a few breeds, judges must do as the Standard tells them.

Probably in the Alsatian, angulation has reached its peak and maybe the Alsatian has not suffered so much as the Gaze-hounds. However, we have a lot of hip dysplasia in Alsatians but there is no evidence that hip dysplasia exists in wolves or foxes, nor that it has made its appearance in zoological gardens where wolves are allowed to live under fairly natural conditions.

There is, however, one thing quite certain, that a shorter, straight leg taking a lot of short, quick strides is superior in speed to the long angulated legs which take longer strides, but fewer of them. All that we have gained in our angulated dogs as my friend, the judge, told me is beauty — at the expense of performance.

In order to judge according to the existing standards, we must look for a well-flexed stifle and a similarly flexed hock. As the two joints work in unison the one guarantees the other.

The only breed in which the stifle and hock must be straight is in the Chow Chow. It is desirable that the hind legs should be muscular in this breed, the hocks well let down and perfectly straight, in order to produce the Chow's characteristic stilted gait. Quite a few Chow Chows become double jointed so that the point of the hock turns forward. The Standard does not mention this, but it is to be presumed it would be regarded as a fault.

In the Bulldog the hind legs are large and muscular, and longer in proportion than the forelegs, so as to elevate the loins. The hocks should only be slightly bent but well let down so that the leg shall appear long and muscular from the loins to the point of the hock. The leg below the hock should be short, straight and strong. The stifles should be round and turned slightly away from the body. This will cause the points of the hocks to approach one another and the hind feet to turn outwards. The forefeet should turn slightly outwards.

It may be imagined that a young judge relying considerably upon what he has been led to regard as soundness and unsoundness, might, if he had not previously read the Standard, turn down a very good Bulldog for what he might wrongly regard as unsoundness.

He will also be on the look out for the characteristic 'roach back'. There should be a slight fall in the back close behind the shoulders. Behind this fall the back will rise to the loins, to a height *above* that of the shoulders, then curve down down more suddenly to the tail, forming an arch.

The tail is characteristic, too.

It (known as 'the stern') should be set on low, jut out rather straight, and then turn downwards. It should be moderate in length, thick at the root, tapering quickly to a fine point. The tail must not be capable of being lifted above the level of the back.

All of which goes to prove that it is essential to read, learn and inwardly digest the Standards of every breed.

In the French Bulldog in a similar fashion, the hind legs must be longer than the forelegs, so as to make the loins higher than the shoulders. In this breed, however, both fore and hind feet must lie straight with the body and there must be none of the cow-hocked appearance as seen in the English Bulldog. The tail is similar in both breeds and is designed so it cannot be carried gaily.

In the Yorkshire Terrier the hind legs including the hocks and stifle should be quite straight.

In the Cavalier, the hind legs must be straight.

In the Maltese the hind limbs are nicely angulated.

6

Movement and Action

Reading show reports constantly leads one to the opinion that at least a few of the modern judges must be blessed with a surprising gift of being able to discern all the little niceties of movement, and of being capable of going over a class of twenty dogs, picking out half-a-dozen which excelled on show points and then sorting these out into the requisite number of placings entirely upon their movement, all in ten minutes.

Such a statement may quite easily raise a flood of protests from exhibitors who do not believe this happens, or that the decision is difficult to make. Let me hasten to add that I am not so concerned with the championship shows. Most of the breed judges concern themselves with movement as they should do, but they assess the conformation and show points and add up these and movement together to get a genuine assessment.

I am referring to the enormous number of small shows in which the judge picks out his best half dozen exhibits and then, according to his own critique, judges them entirely on movement.

I have just checked one or two shows and find that one judge by his own showing, decided all the final places in four classes entirely upon movement. This is no exception in the smaller shows. My point is that if six dogs out of an entry of say fourteen, were all equally good or equally bad on conformation, unless three of the six were cripples, would it be so easy to do this?

I claim from a pretty wide experience of studying movement in dogs of all kinds that the ability to judge movement accurately is less liable to be present in the average all-rounder, than ability to judge show points.

Rightly or wrongly, I regard an accurate assessment of movement as the most difficult of all the feats the judge is called upon to perform. I feel sure that the majority of really experienced judges will agree with me.

My own experience has been gained not in the show ring so much as by the study of gait and movement on so many occasions every day of the week, in the course of my professional duties, and the necessity to distinguish between a very slight peculiarity in gait, and an acquired lameness, which might or might not be amenable to treatment. To make a decision I would need the dog walked and trotted at different paces and then moved in a circle, possibly on more than one occasion. In a few cases I might need the help of an X-ray film, particularly if the abnormality concerned a foot, a hip or a stifle.

All that one could do with six dogs, in ten minutes, would be to make a rough guess as to which was worse than another.

There is a general belief, held even by a few judges, that if a dog is sound in conformation, has a good shoulder, elbows and front, and has sound hips, and stifles, and sound hocks, it. cannot help but travel sound. Unfortunately this is not always the case. Moreover, a few dogs with quite poor conformation may occasionally travel sound, or at least much better than certain other dogs which on grounds of conformation one would expect to go better than they actually do.

There is a reason for this, and it lies not in the anatomical layout but in the dog's nervous system. The fault lies in lack of, or faulty synchronisation of the muscles of the body, and particularly of those controlling the limbs.

In our physiology we are taught that most of the joint movements in animals are controlled by what is known as 'co-operative antagonism of muscles'.

If we consider the forelimb, we see the shoulder joint extended by means of the biceps muscle in front of the joint. When the biceps contracts it extends (straightens) the shoulder joint.

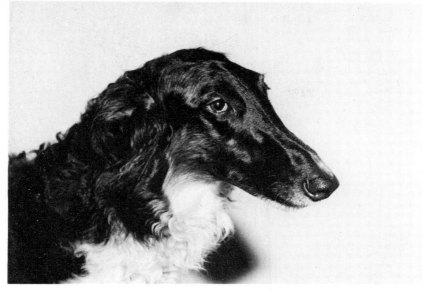

Ch. Black Limelight of Enolan.

BASSET HOUND
Ch. Brackenacre Anabella.
Owner: Marianne Nixon.

FRENCH BULLDOG
Ch. Robindale Chaseholme
Nonpareil.
Owner: Mrs. E. Griffin.

DALMATIAN
Sophia of Ranon
Owner: Miss June Longmuir.

At the back of the limb we have the triceps muscle which flexes (bends) the shoulder joint.

These two antagonistic muscles, the biceps and the triceps, work in harmony as well as at cross purposes. If the forelimb were suddenly thrust forward without any resistance to its own strength, the arm might fracture, so when the shoulder joint is operated, both muscles, the one in front and the one behind it, contract simultaneously. If we wish to flex our own arm, our biceps contracts and also the triceps but we permit the biceps to assume dominance, while the triceps takes care that the biceps does not over-do its job.

This goes on with all the muscles all over the body but especially in those of the limbs.

In the hind limbs we have the gastrocnemius extending (straightening) the hock and stifle, and the flexor metatarsi in front of the limb in opposition, keeping some tension on the joint all the time and preventing strain and ruptures of the muscles or tendons.

All these are operated from their own centres in the brain. There are many muscles operating all at the same time in this way all over the body.

All movement is controlled by muscles, voluntary or in-voluntary. The contraction of the biceps, when we wish to flex our arm, is a voluntary action. That of the triceps is automatic, but it can fail to function, or it may operate completely successfully. If it does not do so the voluntary action of the biceps may be completely disturbed. We use our hands and arms to work with, wash and feed ourselves, dress and undress, for example.

A dog uses its muscles to scratch itself but mainly for purposes of locomotion. If the naturally antagonistic muscle is not performing satisfactorily the dog will show it in its walk.

And yet the conformation of the bones and limbs may be perfect. But the dog is lame or affected with in-coordination, which means that its muscles are not operating in harmony.

Why does this happen? It may be due to a defect in the brain or spinal cord, which may have been present since birth — or it may be left behind by a virus infection, such as distemper. A dog may make a seemingly wonderful recovery from a mild attack of the disease and be quite abnormal in movement ever afterwards, even if structurally it appears perfectly sound.

In rare cases the lack of synchronisation may be due to epilepsy. This does not mean that epilepsy is rare in the dog. The tendency is in fact quite common, but it seldom causes a persistent disorder within the muscles. It can, however, cause some degree of abnormality, particularly when a dog is wound up, or excited, as in the show ring.

Some breeds have familial disorders which are accepted as normal in the breed.

The Bulldog, for example, has a peculiar heavy and constrained gait, appearing to walk with short, quick steps on the tips of its toes, its hind feet being lifted high but appearing to skim the ground. The Bulldog runs also with its right shoulder rather advanced, similarly to a horse when cantering.

The Pyrenean has a rolling, ambling gait, a characteristic which it shares with another breed which originally did similar work guarding flocks.

The Old English Sheepdog when walking or trotting, shows a characteristic ambling or pacing movement which disappears at the gallop.

Italian Greyhounds exhibit a hackney-like high-stepping in front. Some Toy Poodles are apt to move in this way.

In the Black and Tan Terrier high-stepping is forbidden.

The Chow Chow has a stilted gait.

In the Dalmatian there should be a long free stride with the hind legs tracking the forelegs.

The basis of good action lies in the properly inclined scapula.

Although some dogs with upright shoulders appear to move reasonably well they lack the free front limb action and reach of stride that goes with a well-formed shoulder. Moreover, this perfection of forelimb movement can only be achieved when the head is carried high, preferably on top of a long, supple neck, which fits in well with the shoulder beneath it. Unless the head is carried high the brachiocephalic muscle will be unable to pull the humerus and the foreleg forward to its full extent.

To study movement thoroughly it is necessary to watch the dog coming towards you, going away from you, passing you on one side, and then on the other side; and finally travelling in a circle in one direction and then in the other. Obviously there is not time nor space to do all this in a show ring and one has to be content with the dog going away and returning.

Incidentally, as one judge from across the Irish Sea, once remarked to me: 'Very often the best time to see a dog moving is when it's standing still!'

There is some truth in this. Dogs have a habit, when standing, of favouring one foot. Occasionally, one can tell by detecting an atrophied (wasted) shoulder muscle or one in the thigh, when the animal is standing still, that this particular leg does not do its full share of work.

When the dog is standing, notice a turned-in foot, one which is not taking full weight, or a 'dropped' quarter, i.e. one which has a wasted muscle in the quarter, which makes one quarter appear a little lower than the other.

Nails are usually trimmed for show but if they are not, it is frequently an indication of unsoundness when the toenails of one foot are longer than those of its fellow; 'lacking wear'.

Have the dog led away from you, preferably on not too tight a lead. When the dog trots, most judges like to be able to see the pads of all the feet.

Judges of Poodles frequently prefer *not* to see the soles of the *hind* feet when the Poodle trots away.

Similarly, although the stifle and hock need to be bent it is frequently considered desirable by some Poodle judges for the hind feet to fall in line with the seat bones rather than be carried behind the body. This does not appear to be mentioned in the Standard still issued, but it is frequently being put into practice.

As the dog trots away from you take especial notice of its hocks and whether they remain parallel, or if one hock is inclined to knock against the other. The one hock may seem to be doing more work than the other, flexing more, so that the hind movement becomes a hop, skip and jump activity rather than a measured orderly procedure in which both hocks seem to be sharing the burden. There may be several reasons, although the judge must act on what he actually sees without the need to make a diagnosis.

One reason may be a patella on one side (or on both) which slips out of place occasionally, so that sometimes it is on and sometimes it is off. This is more common in small Toys and in Miniature and Toy Poodles.

Another reason may simply be a sore foot. A small cut on a pad, or a piece of grit lodged in some part of the ground surface of the foot, could cause the lameness.

Occasionally a dog flexes one hock more than the other because earlier in life it has had an injury, even a healed fracture.

Lameness becomes a habit sometimes following an injury and it may never show until the dog enters the strained atmosphere in which it has to be on its best behaviour. Then the limp may return.

Pacing and pin-toeing also come into this category.

We will now watch the dog turn round and come back towards us. Note any crossing of the legs during making the turn. A lot will depend on the handler. The anxious novice is quite capable of pulling a shy, awkward puppy right off its feet on the turn.

Watch the head, whether it is carried high and proudly, or if it is low, or even sniffing the ground. There is no law against sniffing the ground but it loses marks. Sometimes a dog may be forgiven in a class containing bitches. The bitch should not be there in all probability.

The two fore legs should be brought well forward from the shoulders and elbows, and they should operate in complete parallel, the one with the other.

Keep an eye on the elbows and note if they press tightly against the side of the chest, or if they are slack and given to 'wobble'.

Note any pintoeing, or the alternative, whether the feet turn out.

84

Observe any tendency to *dish*, which means that the feet do not follow in the line of the limb but turn outwards *when the knee is flexed*. This means that as the dog comes towards you the feet *'swing'* outwards and to the rear.

Another common fault is *plaiting* in which one forefoot is placed exactly in a line with the other forefoot so that there would, in the snow for example, be a single line of footmarks instead of a double line.

If everything else appears correct notice how the foot approaches you, whether it is shuffled along the ground or picked up and put down neatly. You can see this better when the dogs are parading around the ring, with yourself in the middle of it.

Notice the body as the dog goes away from you and observe any tendency to roll, remembering that some breeds are privileged in this respect. Note the topline at the same time and any tendency to hump the back or dip it in the middle, when moving.

You will have noted any tendency to cow-hocks when you made your initial examination.

You will also have examined the scrotum to determine whether the dog, a male, is entire. It is not your job to search for a missing testicle. You have to decide whether the dog has two normal-sized testicles within the scrotum. If one is very large and the other remarkably small; or if one is present and the other cannot be felt *within the scrotum,* the dog is unsound (and under recent ruling this must be regarded as a fault).

If there is a veterinary surgeon attached to the show his attention may be called to it, *privately*, at the judge's discretion.

Testing Alsatians is a specialist's job, although the all-rounder may find it necessary to carry it out when there are two or more 'likely' Alsatians in a variety class.

Alsatians are judged not only on conformation but largely upon movement. Not only is the outstanding lengthy stride of the exhibit and its ability to keep its body parallel with the ground taken into account but also its power of endurance and when this has to be carried out in the confines of a comparatively small hall, the whole procedure becomes a test not only of the physique of the Alsatian, but equally so of that of its handler.

The usual procedure is the running and walking of the dog up and down the ring and then a somewhat prolonged circular run, either inside a very big ring, or preferably in some spacious part of the hall reserved for the purpose. Although the procedure has become customary, how it is carried out must rest a good deal in the hands of the judge and his steward or stewards. There is no set procedure other than the direction that the gait must be supple, smooth and long-reaching, carrying the body along with the minimum of up-and-down movement, entirely free from stiltiness.

7

Weight and Size

Space does not permit a lengthy consideration of every separate breed, nor is this necessary since a full description of each with all the good points as well as the faults, can be obtained from the appropriate breed Standards published by the Kennel Club. The Standards mention certain faults which should be penalised and others regarding which a judge may use his own discretion.

It must not be presumed that the discovery of a fault is fatal to the dog's chances. Every dog has at least one or more minor faults if one likes to be meticulous but there are degrees in faults just as there are in merits. Sometimes it may appear easier to downgrade a dog for a fault than to decide between a couple of exhibits purely on their merits.

Nevertheless, there are certain faults which one can never completely overlook especially when they are of the type which may be handed down and eventually ruin a good strain.

These include certain eye conditions and especially mouth faults. But when penalising one exhibit for a fault, one must make quite sure that one is not overlooking an even worse fault, not so obvious, in a dog that is being placed above the original offender.

One could so easily penalise one dog for a slightly wry or undershot mouth and put over it one that was completely deaf without being aware of it, because deafness is not always obvious without tests one could not use, or might not be permitted to use, in a ring, and then only by a qualified veterinary surgeon.

One can imagine an Any Variety Class, Bred by the Owner, which contained a white Bull Terrier completely deaf, a black Toy Poodle with perfectly good-looking eyes that were completely blind, an Old English Sheepdog which had been castrated, and a good Great Dane with a slightly undershot mouth.

Probably it will never happen — but it could.

One of the fixed points set out by the Kennel Club is in connection with size and weight. I do not think that one need be too particular as regards the odd inch or ounce but the fact remains that when two dogs are equal in merit and one is considerably overweight or obviously oversized, it must give way to the dog which conforms with the Standard. In some breeds, Whippets for instance, the Standard says that if an exhibit is good in every other way the judge may be permitted to stretch a point in the matter of size. One might feel generous in respect to a bitch, a prospective dam, which was slightly large, or a shade long in body, but one might not regard a male in the same way.

To weigh a dog in the ring is not to be thought of, but measurement is not so difficult and is commonly practised in Toy Poodles, for example. In order that the judge may have some indication as to the weights and measurements laid down for each breed, I am including a set of tables which may possibly give a general idea of weights and inches permissible.

A TABLE OF WEIGHTS AND MEASURES

D means Dog   B means Bitch

BREED	WEIGHT (in pounds)	HEIGHT (in inches)
The Hound Group AFGHAN		D 27-29 B 2-3 in. smaller
BASENJI	D 24 B 21	D 17 B 16

BREED	WEIGHT (in pounds)	HEIGHT (in inches)
BASSET HOUND		13-15
BEAGLE		13-16
BLOODHOUND	D 110 B 100	D 25-27 B 23-35
BORZOI		D 29 plus B 27 plus
DACHSHUND (Smooth) (Wirehaired) (Longhaired) Miniature (Longhaired) (Smooth)	D up to 25 B up to 23 D 20-22 B 18-20 D up to 18 B up to 17 Not over 11 Not over 11	
DEERHOUND	D 85-105 B 65-80	D not under 30 B not under 28
ELKHOUND	D $20\frac{1}{2}$ B $19\frac{1}{2}$	D 50 B 43
FINNISH SPITZ		D $17\frac{1}{2}$ B $15\frac{1}{2}$ Length of body D 20 B 18
GREYHOUND		D 28-30 B 27-28

BREED	WEIGHT (in pounds)	HEIGHT (in inches)
RHODESIAN RIDGEBACK	D 80 B 70 Up or down	D 25-27 B 24-26
SALUKI	5	D 23-28 B proportionately smaller
WHIPPET		D 18½ B 17½ Exercise discretion
Working Group ALSATIAN		D 24-26 B 22-24
BEARDED COLLIE		D 21-22 B 20-21
BOXER	D about 66 B about 62	D 22-24 B 21-23
BULLMASTIFF	D 110-130 B 90-110	D 25-27 B 24-26
COLLIE	D 45-65 B 40-55	D 22-24 B 20-22
DOBERMANN		D 27 B 25½
GREAT DANE	D 30 plus B 28 plus	D 120 B 100

BREED	WEIGHT (in pounds)	HEIGHT (in inches)
NEWFOUNDLAND	D 140-150 B 110-120	D 28 B 26
O. E. SHEEPDOG		D 22 plus B slightly less
PYRENEAN MOUNTAIN DOG	D 100-125 B 90-115	D 27-35 B 25-29 Girth D 36-42 B 32-36
ROTTWEILER	D 25-27 B 23-25	
ST. BERNARD	D The greater the better B	
SAMOYED		D 20-22 B 18-20
SHETLAND SHEEPDOG		D 14½ B 14
WELSH CORGI (Cardigan) (Pembroke)	D 22-26 B 20-24 D 20-24 B 18-22	12 at shoulder 10-12 at shoulder
Utility Group BOSTON TERRIER	Lightweight 15 Middleweight 15-20 Heavyweight 20-25	
BULLDOG	D 55 B 50	

BREED	WEIGHT (in pounds)	HEIGHT (in inches)
CHOW CHOW		18 plus
DALMATIAN		23-24
FRENCH BULLDOG	D 28 B 24	D 23-24 B 22-23
POODLE (Standard) Miniature Toy		15 and over Not under 11 but under 15 Under 11
KEESHOND		D 18 B 17
SCHIPPERKE	12-16	
SCHNAUZER Miniature		D 19 B 18 More than one inch variation penalised D 14 B 13
SHIH TZU	9-18	
TIBETAN APSO	D 9-10 Bitches slightly smaller	
TIBETAN SPANIEL	D 10-16 B 9-15	D up to 11 B up to 9½

BREED	WEIGHT (in pounds)	HEIGHT (in inches)
TIBETAN TERRIER		D 14-16 B Slightly smaller
The Terrier Group AIREDALE		D 23-24 B 22-23
AUSTRALIAN TERRIER	10-11	10
BEDLINGTON	18-23	16
BORDER TERRIER		D 13-15½ B 11½-14
BULL TERRIER Miniature	Not over 20	Not over 14
BULL TERRIER	No Standard weight or size Impression of maximum substance to size of dog.	
CAIRN	14	
DANDIE DINMONT	18	8-11
FOX TERRIER (Smooth)	D 16-18 B	16-18
(Wire)	D 18 B 16	D Not over 15½ B Proportion- ately less

BREED	WEIGHT (in pounds)	HEIGHT (in inches)
IRISH TERRIER	D 27 B 25	18
KERRY BLUE	D 33-37 B 35	D 18-19 B Proportion-ately less
LAKELAND TERRIER	D 17 B 15	14½
MANCHESTER TERRIER		D 16 B 15
NORFOLK and NORWICH TERRIERS		10
SCOTTISH TERRIER	19-23	10-11
SEALYHAM TERRIER	D Not over 20 B Not over 18	Not over 12
SKYE TERRIER	D 25 B Slighty less	10 Total length 41½
STAFFORDSHIRE BULL TERRIER	D 28-38 B 24-34	14-16
WELSH TERRIER	20-21	15½
WEST HIGHLAND WHITE		11

BREED	WEIGHT (in pounds)	HEIGHT (in inches)
Gundog Group		
ENGLISH SETTER	D 60-66 B 56-62	D $25\frac{1}{2}$-27 B 24-$25\frac{1}{2}$
GORDON SETTER	About 56	D 26 B $24\frac{1}{2}$
GERMAN SHORT- HAIRED POINTER	D 55-70 B 45-60	D 23-25 B $24\frac{1}{2}$
RETRIEVER Curly Coated Flat Coated GOLDEN	70-80 60-70 D 65-70 B 55-60	25-27 D 22-24 B 20-22
LABRADOR		D 22-$22\frac{1}{2}$ B $21\frac{1}{2}$-22
The Spaniels		
CLUMBER	D 55-70 B 45-60	
COCKER	D 28-32	D $15\frac{1}{2}$-16 B 15-$15\frac{1}{2}$
FIELD	35-40	About 18
IRISH WATER SPANIEL		D 21-23 B 20-22
ENGLISH SPRINGER	Approx. 50	Approx. 20
SUSSEX	D 45 B 40	15-16

BREED	WEIGHT (in pounds)	HEIGHT (in inches)
WEIMERANER	D 55-65 B 45-55	D 23-25 B 45-55
Toy Group CHIHUAHUA	2-4, up to 6 The smaller the better	
ENGLISH TOY TERRIER	6-8	10-12
GRIFFON BRUXELLOIS	3-10 6-9 preferable	
ITALIAN GREYHOUND	6-8, never over 10	
JAPANESE	Under or over 7	
CAVALIER	10-11	
KING CHARLES SPANIEL	8-14	
MALTESE		Not over 10 inches
MINIATURE PINSCHER		10-12
PAPILLON		8-11
PEKINGESE	D 7-11 B 8-12	

BREED	WEIGHT (in pounds)	HEIGHT (in inches)
POMERANIAN	D 4 -4½ B 4½-5½	
PUG	14-18	
YORKSHIRE TERRIER	Up to 7	

8

Conclusion

Before I close down, please let me emphasise that I have not written this book with the intention of teaching our present judges. We have a great many excellent ones, of both sexes, from whom I would be pleased to accept advice, rather than offer it to them.

But unfortunately, most of these judges, many of whom are my personal friends, all seem to be in one age group, and there must come a day when their advice will be extremely valuable but they will no longer feel capable of travelling all over this country, and many others, and maintaining the pace associated with frequent judging engagements at the largest shows.

It is to be hoped that a number of our younger exhibitors will graduate during the next decade as judges, commencing at the smaller shows, preferably as judges of the one or two breeds they have exhibited, and are most capable of judging.

There is, however, a feeling in some circles that exhibitors do not always make the best judges of the All Round variety; that they may quite naturally favour the strains they have been associated with, and that they may have so many friends to whom they are indebted; people who have advised and helped them in the days when they were beginners themselves; that it would be difficult to remain unaware of the existence when one attains a position in which it would be easy to repay past kindness.

We must presume, of course, that our budding judge is highly conscientious and that he, or she, would not be influenced in the slightest; but human nature being what it is, certainly makes life more difficult.

Again, a young judge, afraid of making some ghastly mistake which may bring about his downfall, is inclined to believe that the people with the big names must necessarily possess the best exhibits. Sometimes they do, but some are apt to produce some 'not-so-good' for a leg-up on occasion, particularly when the judge is not highly experienced.

Young judges should always start work in a strange neighbourhood where the exhibits and exhibitors are all unknown to them. They could not then be influenced in any degree by past knowledge of the dogs or their owners. If they are not capable of handling such a situation they clearly are in need of further tuition.

Where can one get it? I can only reiterate what I said about outside classes sponsored by those who offer 'Further Education'; or by private enterprise. One of the difficulties is to provide material, and this could only be negotiated by co-operation with the owners of established kennels.

It becomes increasingly clear that as things are at present, a knowledge of dogs can only be acquired either by breeding dogs or by working in a number of kennels in order to get experience of a variety of breeds. Presuming that the student provides himself with all the relevant Standards and studies them religiously, this may be as good a way as any.

On the other hand, now that good salaries are easy to come by in situations in which dogs are never mentioned, one may seriously inquire what are the prospects of a young man who wishes to take up judging as a profession? The answer is, 'Not Good!'

The smaller shows cannot afford to pay respectable fees plus travelling expenses, and the larger shows want more highly experienced judges.

Shows are held usually on a Saturday with an occasional mid-week event. Sunday shows are beginning to materialise.

At the commencement, at any rate, judging can be only an occasional or part-time job for someone who is fully engaged the remainder of the week in some other occupation.

Moreover, as judging appointments may be a hundred or more miles from home and judging may start as early as 10 a.m., getting there on time may mean travelling by night and home again by night, after a hard day's work, with the alternative of hotel accommodation which will cost as much as the judge is likely to earn on the trip.

Now can the reader see why I am wondering where the next generation of first class judges will come from? And why I consider that in the interests of this very popular Fancy some official body should provide means of tuition.

It must be recognised that the future of the Dog Fancy, like its past, lies completely in the hands of the judging profession.

A good many years ago now, the last World War depleted the Fancy of most of its breeding stock. When the war came to an end and showing could begin in earnest, we had very few dogs and practically all the 'good' ones had died or been put to sleep as there was no food available for more than the occasional dog.

In a little over twenty years we again have dogs fit to compete with those from all over the world, if it were possible (as unfortunately it isn't) to bring them together.

The rapid recovery has been due partly to the enthusiastic response made by breeders and exhibitors, but chiefly to the fact that we retained a number of highly efficient judges, mainly the old all-rounders, who knew their jobs, judged according to the Standards, and out of inferior stock have now selected potential sires and dams, which have bred even better dogs than we had prior to the War.

We are fortunate in having some of these judges with us today but at risk of offending a few people, I must say that when a score or more of these go into retirement, we have very few up-and-coming judges who would be able to step into their shoes and carry on the wonderful work that these men and women have done. At present we are bringing over into this country a considerable number of foreign judges, but it is to be hoped that this will not be our ultimate solution.

What a pity we cannot apprentice potential judges to some of these outstanding British judges as students, in the guise of Stewards!

For the welfare of the Fancy and its future, all young judges must be persuaded to study the existing Standards and make their awards to exhibits which come nearest to their requirements. It is true that many of these Standards are not very complete and some could do with revision, but on the whole they indicate the type of dog required and it is better to work according to the Standards than to indulge in original ideas.

In several other countries prospective judges are trained, examined and licensed, then put on trial for a stated period. But judging in other countries is rather different to what it is in our own land. Here we have sanction shows, open shows, championship shows and shows for special breeds.

We are a dog-loving race and we have a large number of exhibitors as compared with our population. The Sanction shows weed out the hopeless from the fairly good and the Open shows pick the future possible champions out of the rank and file. At our larger shows every exhibit is a dog of high standard and only the very experienced judge can attempt to place them in their true order.

In many other countries the general standard is not so high and the really good dogs stand out so that their selection is not beyond the skill of the trained judge.

There is one other judging procedure which calls for comment. This is the Best in Show, which at Championship events is usually left to a single judge, one who has not participated in the general judging.

This might be satisfactory if the chosen person knew all the breeds and was capable of making his award upon the very fine points which might make one very good dog of a certain breed a shade better than another very good dog of another breed. One might be a Great Dane or a Newfoundland, the other a Shih Tzu.

The general public, those who take any interest in dogs, are confident that the actual judging for Best in Show may be a farce. They feel, in the first place, that the person appointed is quite often not qualified to make the decision and that the award is made not to a particular dog but to a particular breed, one which certain sections of the Fancy would like to become popular.

This is as it may be, but a good many ringsiders, including the writer, are of the opinion that the choice of breed should play no part and that the actual decision should be made by more than one judge. Two might be sufficient, provided they were both recognised all-rounders of repute and that they made their decision after complete examination, without reference to the judges who originally made the awards.

In conclusion may I express the hope that some of the younger exhibitors will appreciate what is an evident fact, that there is likely to be a scarcity of capable judges comparable with those of today, within the next ten or fifteen years.

If anything I have written in this volume may encourage some of them to enter the ranks, and particularly if it has helped them to appreciate the anatomical features which are the basis of breed characteristics, my labours will not have been in vain.

Appendix

A breed summary for and against

To be read in conjunction with each Breed Standard
THE HOUND GROUP
AFGHAN HOUND
For: Oriental expression. Gait and carriage; head carried high, long stride with feet well lifted. Long forehead, long jaws, prominent occiput. Long sloping shoulder, tight elbows. Level back, fairly long; loin wide but short. Prominent hips. Big feet covered with hair. Tail lifted during movement with ring at end. Hair on back short along spine.
Against: Coarseness. Skull too narrow or too wide. Straight shoulder. Crooked front and weak elbows. Short neck. Poor coat. Faulty mouth. Tired or lazy movement.
BASENJI
For: Flat, wrinkled head. Sharp pointed ears, slightly turning to centre. Curved, rather flattened neck continuous with a sloping shoulder. Rather long pasterns with small narrow, bunched feet. Appearing rather high on leg. Tail set very high, curling tightly over the spine and finally resting on the thigh.
Against: Round skull, or occiput too marked. Bad mouth. Large round eye; barrel chest. Ears too large. Low on leg. Dewlap.
BASSET HOUND
For: Short legs without impaired movement. Long front stride and good hind limb propulsion. Domed skull with prominent occiput, lean foreface. Moderate wrinkle on brows. Heavy flews in upper jaw which must not be too wide. Rather slack skin. Ears set level with eyes, curling inwards and reaching end of muzzle. Fairly long neck with dewlap; well-marked

keel. Stop well defined. Wide, open nostrils. Level back, raised a little over loins. Inclined shoulder. Forelegs bent at knees with wrinkling of overlying skin. Very large feet, well knuckled-up. Stifles and hocks bent.

Against: Knees knocking together either when at rest or moving. Tail carried over back. General coarseness of build. Light eyes, too deeply set. Flat chest. Excessive hind angulation. Bad mouth. Short neck. Absence of dewlap. Too short back.

BEAGLE

For: A squarely-built hound, powerful but never coarse. Head with peak and evident stop, fairly wide muzzle and upper lips flewed. Ears low and reaching almost to nose. Chest deep over a moderately lengthy foreleg. Ribs wider above than below especially between elbows. Neck fairly long and arched. Stifles and hocks bent but not overangulated. Tail of moderate length carried gaily. Back straight and shorter than in Basset Hound. Loins powerful and slightly raised.

Against: General coarseness; too high or too low on leg. Too long in back. Short neck. Hind feet carried too far behind body. Straight shoulder. Too short in head and too narrow in muzzle. Bad mouth. Large prominent eyes.

BLOODHOUND

For: Head long and narrow with prominent peak. The narrowness is continued down the muzzle so that the head seems to be flattened from side to side. Foreface square in outline. Whole of head carries an excess of loose skin in folds and wrinkles. The eyes have the lower lids pulled down with the eyes seemingly buried in their sockets. The body is long with the neck carried in a straight line ahead, seeming to add to its length. The skin of neck and body also profuse and can be raised by hand a foot above neck level. Ribs well sprung and chest deep. Tail carried level with back. Well inclined shoulder, straight forelegs with strong, not overlarge, well-knuckled feet. Muscular second thighs, stifles and hocks well-bent and hocks close to ground. Ears thin and very long, set on low and falling gracefully.

Against: Quarrelsome. Lack of free-swinging gait. Thick skull. Eyelashes interfering with eye surface. Weak bone.

BORZOI

For: A dog with a romantic, aristocratic appearance. Characterised by speed, length of jaw and a beautiful flat or waved coat. The head is very long and finely chiselled with dark, elliptical eyes and absence of the stop, so that the face presents a 'Roman nosed' appearance, levelling out into a long, straight and tapering muzzle. The ears are small and fine, folded back like those of a greyhound. Forelegs long, straight, and well-boned over long, narrow, slightly-arched feet. Body is deep and flat-sided in its lower half particularly in the elbow region but well sprung in its upper half. Well-ribbed body. Strong loins. The back is slightly arched. Hind limbs bent at stifles and hocks and well-angulated.

Against: Light eyes. Too straight in shoulder. Cow-hocks. Mouth with teeth not level. Out-at-elbows. Forelimbs too wide apart above, and forelegs not perpendicular.

DACHSHUNDS

The smallest of the Hound Group but with smooth, rough and wire-haired, and smooth, and long-haired miniature varieties. The difference lies in coat, otherwise all are similar.

For: Head long, tapering, slightly rounded between ears which are set high and well back. Muzzle rather long and pointed. Mouth wide and extending back behind eye level. Eyes almond shape and obliquely set. Back long, straight but slightly raised at loins. Upright neck and head carried high. Front broad between arms with rather prominent keel. Legs very short, but well-boned with slight crook between the two forelegs, faintly resembling those of a Chippendale·chair, but without any degree of exaggeration. Scapula well sloped.

The body is long with ribs carried far back and the belly lightly drawn up behind their termination. The length of the body from front of keel to the root of the tail equals twice that from withers to the ground.

The stern is set fairly high and should be wide and well muscled. The tail should curl back above ground level.

Movement is very important and as it is a weak spot in this breed, it should be given a deal of attention.

The Smooth Dachshund has a smooth, glossy flat coat in black-and-tan, red, liver, chocolate, brindle, tiger marked, or dapple. White is forbidden except a small white spot on breast. Nose and nails black though a red dog may have a red nose though it is not desirable. In Chocolates and Dapples the nose may be brown or flesh-coloured. The dappling must not be too pronounced or the spots too large, even dappling with small or medium spots, is preferred. Dogs, 25 lbs maximum. Bitches, 23 lbs.

The Long-haired Dachshund is one of the early varieties possibly with some Setter or Spaniel blood introduced. Similar to the smooth variety apart from its long, soft coat which is straight or slightly wavy. It provides abundant feathering behind the legs, below the neck and abdomen and should be well displayed in the tail.

Medium. Dogs, 18 lbs. Bitches 17 lbs.

Heavyweight; up to approximately 25 lbs.

The Wire-haired Dachshund. As this is used as a tracking dog and well adapted to going to ground the mouth must be particularly good and powerful with scissor bite. Body completely covered with a short, even, wire coat, harsh outside with a good undercoat. The usual colours are permitted as in the smooth variety. The ears are usually smooth and soft with the eyebrows very bushy.

Dogs, 20-22 lbs. Bitches, 18-20 lbs.

Miniature Long-haired Dachshund. Small, but game, very active and intelligent. Movement requires watching, especially as 'plaiting' is common, while the hind legs may be thrown from side to side when moving. Mouth must be true, neither under nor over-shot. The eyes should be small, oblique, and never protruding. Weight not over 11 lbs.

Miniature Smooth-haired Dachshund. A smaller edition of the normal smooth Dachshund. Must not exceed 11 lbs, and must not be woolly or curly coated.

Miniature Wire-haired Dachshund. A smaller replica of the larger wire-haired type. Weight must not exceed 11 lbs.

Common faults in Dachshunds: Round heads; full, rounded and prominent eyes. Roach back. Under or overshot mouths. Hollow back dipping behind shoulders. Loose elbows. Feet turning in. Cow-hocks and irregular hind action. Short neck and upright shoulder. Legs too long. Belly excessively tucked-up. Splayed feet with weak pads. Chest too flat. Sternum touching the ground. Breast bone abnormally prominent.

GREYHOUND

For: Noted for beauty and symmetry. Head cleanly cut with tapering muzzle, moderately wide between ears. Flat forehead with hardly any stop. Ears, small, rose-shaped, lying back on neck during repose.

Chest deep and capacious, not barrel-shaped. Ribs carried well back with cut-up flanks. Back rather long with powerful loin, slightly arched. Long sloping shoulder with long straight forelegs. Hindquarters continuous with thigh when galloping. Long muscular second thigh, hocks set low and well bent. Feet moderate in length and well knuckled. Tail long and fine, set low, slightly curved but not lifted above horizontal.

Against: Barrel chest, upright shoulder, short neck. Back too arched throughout. Straight hocks. Weak pasterns. Weak loin. Light eyes.

IRISH WOLFHOUND

For: In size midway between Deerhound and Great Dane. Head long but skull not broad. Long, moderately pointed muzzle. Dark eyes. Ears flat on neck until aroused. Long muscular arched neck. Muscular shoulder, well sloped. Long back with arched loins. Deep chest. Long second thighs, and hocks well bent. Belly well tucked-up. Rather large, round feet. Tail long, slightly curved and well-covered with fur.

Against: Untypical head with Roman nose. Dewlap. Hollow back or back too short.

THE ELKHOUND

A compact, short-bodied dog with a thick and abundant coat of coarse but soft texture, not bristling but very weather-resistant. Head broad between ears. Visible stop but not over-stressed. Forehead and top of head slightly arched. Muzzle tapering from its base but not pointed. Strong jaw with firm, closed lips.

Dark eyes, round but not prominent. Ears erect, a little higher than wide, pointed and active. Neck not too long and not over-short, curving down to withers. Must be thick and muscular.

Body short in coupling, deep from withers to sternum. Ribs full and well-rounded, thick short loin with tail set high and curled tightly over loin, covered in short, thick hair. Back straight and abdomen not tucked-up. Hindquarters very muscular with straight stifles and hocks.

Feet straight, oval and compact.

Colour. Hairs grey with black tips, lighter on chest, stomach, legs and beneath tail. Black patches undesirable. A distinct ruff around neck and front of chest.

THE FINNISH SPITZ

For: A hunting dog with characteristic energy and eagerness. Medium sized, red in colour with prick ears and a large bushy tail curled tightly over back. Head medium in thickness with rather domed skull and a very evident stop, which is continued up between and above the eyes as a rather wide furrow, resulting in a 'foxy' appearance. The eyes are dark and of medium size. The ears resemble those of the Elkhound but can be laid forwards or back at will. Body straight and powerful with deep chest and the belly slightly drawn up. Forelegs straight and of reasonable length for activity, the hindlimbs straight as in the Elkhound.

Against: Dirty colour, dew claws on hind feet, yellow or wall-eyes, badly shaped tail, ears directed too far backwards or forward or outwards.

RHODESIAN RIDGEBACK

For: Characterised by a ridge of hair, directed forward, along centre of back from behind the shoulder to the hips, comprising two identical crowns, opposite each other. At the withers it terminates in a crescentic flourish with the convacity forward. Head broad, flat across top with definite stop. Round, dark eyes. Triangular ears, set high and tapering to a rounded tip, carried close to side of head. Body slightly arched over croup. Deep capacious chest. Large round feet. Tail undocked, tapering and carried low.

Against: Absence or poor development of the ridge.

SALUKI

Characterised by grace, symmetry, speed and endurance. Long, narrow head, rather wide between ears without dome. Stop not apparent. Large, oval, dark eyes. Long mobile ears, covered with long silky hair, hanging close to skull. Shoulder well inclined. Chest deep but not too wide. Lengthy neck. Back broad with hip bones set wide apart. Stifle and hocks bent, hocks low to ground. Tail set on low, curved, with fringe of hair on underside.

WHIPPET

For: Like the Greyhound, a picture of elegance and grace. A long, lean-headed dog with a long neck, a beautifully laid shoulder, moderately long back with a definite arch over the loin, but never a humped back. The chest deep, with spring of rib high up in the rib, but flatter below, so as not to impede the free use of arms and elbows.

A sound straight front with strong pasterns permitting some slight spring, and neat feet well split up between the toes. The hindquarters strong and broad across the thighs, long strong second thighs, well bent stifles and hocks. The second thighs continuous, as it were, with the loin, so that during galloping the back and loins work together to carry the hind feet well forward even in front of the fore feet.

Against: A short neck, upright shoulder, too short or too long a back; a back humped from the withers back, straight stifles and hocks. Flat feet. A kinked tail, or one that goes over the back. Tied-in elbows, or elbows so slack that the walk is pin-toed. A mincing or dancing front action. General coarseness and lack of quality.

THE WORKING GROUP

ALSATIAN

For: A highly intelligent dog with character, personality and a definite presence. Head rather broad, tapering to a fairly sharp but powerful muzzle. Dark eyes. Ears set high, erect and pointed, wide at the base. Moderately long neck, well arched. No definite stop. The shoulder is long and well-sloped in order to give free front action. Forelegs perfectly straight; the pasterns sloping very slightly. Chest deep but ribs a little flat, rather than a chest too broad. Slightly arched loins with croup falling away slightly. Long strong second thighs with well bent stifles and hocks well-angulated to give the characteristic loping action. Feet round with well-arched toes. Tail slightly curved, reaching to hock; never carried above horizontal.

Against: Long, narrow head. Overshot mouth. Liver or pink nose. Pronounced curl in tail. Absence of heavy undercoat. Upright shoulder. Lack of hind angulation. Inefficient movement.

BEARDED COLLIE

Lighter than the Bobtail with plenty of daylight underneath. A free mover. Broad flat skull, drop ears. Long bushy tail. Medium length muzzle, moderately tapered. Eyebrows covered with shaggy hair. Ears medium in size, covered with long hair and drooping. Neck arched and of medium length. Level back and strong loins. Deep, well sprung chest. Sloping shoulders and straight front. Muscular thighs with stifles and hocks well bent. Oval feet, arched. Tail carried gaily when excited but never curled over back. Top coat shaggy; soft, close undercoat. Coat grows right down to feet. Short hair on ridge of nose with a beard hanging from the sides of the upper jaw. Some long hair grows from beneath lower jaw.

BOXER

For: A square smooth-haired dog of strong build, carrying a lot of muscle. Head very accurately modelled. Top of skull slightly arched without marked occiput. There is a deep stop between the forehead (which carries a central furrow) and the upper jaw. The length of the upper jaw from stop to nose equals one third of the length of the whole head. The furrow must not be deep between the eyes. The nose is a little elevated at its tip. The mouth is normally a little undershot and the lower jaw protrudes slightly beyond the upper and in so doing tilts upward, remaining fairly broad in the uplifted portion. There should be six incisors in either jaw. The eyes should be dark brown with a dark rim. Folds from the root of the nose run downwards on either side of the muzzle. The muzzle is a dark mask in distinction with the rest of the face. The muzzle must be powerful, both in direction and height. The cheeks must be well-developed. The ears are thin, set on wide apart and lying close to the cheek. The chest is deep and the ribs wide but not barrel-shaped. The distance from the top of the withers to the breastbone equals the distance from the breastbone to the ground. The body is a little higher at the withers and the back slopes a little downwards at the croup, especially when the dog is on the alert. The shoulder slopes gracefully with stout, strong forelegs and small tightly arched cat-feet. The hind feet are slightly longer than the fore. The hindquarters are very strong with long thighs and well-bent stifles and hocks.

Against: Any tendency to viciousness or unreliable temperament. Built too closely on Bulldog lines. Dewlap. Showing teeth or tongue. Light eyes. Faulty ears. Roach back. Straight hocks. Disproportionate head. Extra incisors.

BULLMASTIFF

A large, heavy but very active dog. Head large and broad; skull flat on top with well-developed cheeks and some wrinkle. Eyes wide apart, medium size with a furrow between. Moderately large triangular ears, set high and lying close at side of cheeks. Muzzle deep and broad and unlike that of the Bulldog. Mouth level, slightly undershot permitted (but disliked). Powerful sloping shoulders. Chest very deep. Wide, muscular loins and powerful thighs. Hocks moderately bent. Tail set high, thick at root and tapering to hocks, carried horizontally when dog is alerted but not over back.

COLLIE (ROUGH)

An intelligent dog of great beauty coupled with agility, on aristocratic lines. Skull flat, fairly wide between ears, tapering towards the eyes and continuing at the muzzle in an unbroken line to the nose, which must be neither snipy nor showing looseness of the lips. A slight almost imperceptible stop. Medium-sized eyes, set obliquely and dark in colour, except in merles. Ears fairly wide apart, not too closely together on top of head, looking forward. In repose they are thrown back but at the alert are brought forward and carried semi-erect with the tips drooping.

Fairly long, rather arched neck. Sloping shoulders. Body rather long, thick behind shoulders with deep chest and well-sprung ribs.

THE DOBERMANN

A medium sized, very active dog, muscular and elegant. Capable of great speed. Highly intelligent. Good tempered and obedient. A good, light and elastic mover.

Head. Long, fine and well-filled below eyes. Wedge shaped tapering with only a slight stop. Flat on top with muzzle parallel with top of skull. Nose black in black dogs, dark brown in brown dogs and dark grey in blue dogs. Eyes rather deeply set, almond shape (never round). In black dogs eyes must be very dark but in lighter coloured dogs the iris must be a little darker than the hair colour. Ears small and set high on head. May be erect or may droop at their tips but erect preferred. Well developed, strong mouth with scissor bite.

Neck erect, fairly long and lean, slightly arched. No dewlap. Shoulder very well-inclined, long upper arm, forelimbs parallel and straight with elbows firmly held to sides. Body square, its height equalling its length. Topline slopes slightly from withers to croup. Abdomen well tucked-up. Stifle and hock well bent, lengthy tibia and perpendicular from heel to hock. Tail docked at first or secont joint. Coat smooth, short and thick and close lying. Feet catlike, compact and well-arched.

Movement is very important. There must be a free forward stride in front compatible with a well-sloped shoulder. The hind drive must be straight and powerful with some rotary movement of the hindquarters.

THE GREAT DANE

A large dog which may attain 120 lbs weight and yet appear lightly built, a free mover with great agility. An elegant

YORKSHIRE TERRIER
Ch. Ravaldene Graybet Rhapsody in Blue.
Owner: Mrs. V. Ravald.

Truxillo Prince Consort.
Owner: Mrs. Motherwell.

WELSH CORGI
Ch. Evancoyd April Love.
Owner: Mrs. Beryl J. Thompson.

TIBETAN SPANIEL
Ch. Braeduke Tam-Cho.
Owner: Mrs. Madeline
Harper.

animal in every way. Head resembles an oblong block set on edge. It may measure up to 13 inches from nose to occiput. The skull is flat, long and narrow with a slight indentation running up its midline. Above the eyes the brows are prominent but there is no marked stop between them. Ears of medium size, triangular and pendant. The foreface is long, equal to the length of the skull, and it terminates perpendicularly to provide a square jaw with tight lips and no flews. The cheeks should lie flat. The head is carried high on an upright neck, long, clean and muscular. The nose is large, and black in self-coloured and brindle dogs. The eyes are not very large for the size of the head; round and dark in fawn and brindle dogs.

The neck runs into withers a little above back level and from these the back travels in a straight line to the croup, and then slightly downward to a stout tail set on rather high, but never raised above back level.

The body has a deep chest reaching within the elbows, with well-rounded ribs. The forelegs are perfectly straight down to the feet. The hindlegs have broad and muscular thighs with hocks and stifles well bent but the feet do not rest a great distance behind. There is a definite tendency in Great Danes to hind limb weakness. This is common in youth but should disappear by the fifteenth month. The feet are well arched and catlike and turn neither in nor out.

The coat is dense, short, sleek and close lying. Colours may be brindles, fawns, blues, blacks and harlequins. Blacks may carry a white spot on brisket or feet and brisket in this country but on the Continent a white front and blaze with a black body are admired. Harlequins are almost a separate variety and not all are up to Standard. The black patches are irregular, up to four inches in diameter and may include the greater part of a limb. The nose may be pink or flesh-coloured; the eyes dark, blue, flesh-coloured, or wall or even odd, or in mixed colours. Blue Danes may have rather light eyes. In all colours the minimum height for a dog is 30 inches, and for a bitch 28 inches.

MASTIFF

A large, solid, powerful dog with an appearance of grandeur. Skull broad between ears with flat forehead and moderate wrinkling especially when roused. Rather high brows with well developed temporal muscles and masseters, producing a rounded head surface and prominent cheeks. There is a depression halfway up the midline of the forehead commencing between the eyes. The muzzle keeps almost as wide as the skull above it, right to the nose where it is squarely cut off, overlying a broad lower jaw. Length of muzzle to whole length of head is as 1 : 3. Circumference of muzzle to that of head is as 3 : 5. Small eyes, wide apart with marked stop. Ears continue the head width, set high and lying flat on the cheeks.

Teeth do not show when mouth is closed.

Chest wide and deep, well let down between elbows. Well arched, rounded ribs, carried well back with girth considerably greater than height at shoulder. Shoulder sloping, legs straight and wide apart. Heavy bone. Upright pasterns. Second thighs long and well-developed. Stifle and hock bent but not excessively angulated. The dog should stand and walk squarely.

Colours. Muzzle, ears and nose black with pigmentation around eyes. Body colour: apricot, silver, fawn or dark fawn—brindle.

NEWFOUNDLAND

A heavy, free-moving dog possessing great strength and marked activity, with a rather rolling gait.

Head broad and massive with a marked occiput. No definite stop. Muzzle short and square covered with short fine hair. Eyes small, deeply set, wide apart and dark brown in colour. Ears small to medium. Triangular, high set and hanging pendant alongside the head.

Neck short, thick and muscular.

Inclined scapula. Body well ribbed, chest deep and fairly broad (for a swimming dog).

Forelegs straight and heavily boned, elbows tight to sides. Hindquarters very strong. Stifles and hocks moderately bent, without dewclaws on hind feet. Feet large and well shaped.

Tail reaches a little below hocks, must not rise above back level.

Coat flat and dense, somewhat oily in texture. Colour, usually black. A slight tinge of bronze or white on chest or toes not objectionable. May be any other colour, white and bronze especially. The Landseer Newfoundland is black and white or bronze and black and tan. In other respects it is identical with the Newfoundland.

OLD ENGLISH SHEEPDOG

The Bobtail is a medium height, strong, compact dog, with a profuse coat in any shade of grey, grizzle, blue or blue merle, with or without white markings.

Its head is large and square, well arched over the eyes and the whole more or less hidden by hair. Jaws strong, moderately long and square. Well defined stop. Large black nose. Eyes dark or wall. Ears small and carried flat on side of head.

Neck fairly long and arched. Forelegs straight and well boned, but not overlong. Sloping shoulder. The body is short and compact, higher over loins and rump than at the withers. Deep, well-ribbed chest. Loins well developed and slightly arched. Hindquarters very rounded and muscular with bobbed tail (normal or docked). A lot of extra coat over hindquarters. Shaggy and free from curl. Waterproof, thick, undercoat.

Colour: Grey, grizzle, blue or blue merle, with or without white markings. Brown or sable objectionable.

Moves with a rolling gait at moderate speeds but gallops freely.

PYRENEAN MOUNTAIN DOG

A majestic dog of great size and intelligence. All white, or with markings of grey, badger, or tan. Up to 32 inches in dogs and 29 inches in bitches. The length and height are the same.

Large wedge-shaped head resembling that of a Brown Bear; up to 11 inches in length. Rounded crown with only slight furrow and no stop. Cheeks flat and lips edged with black, fitting tightly around mouth. Lips and around eyelids pigmented. Eyes set obliquely, dark rich brown in colour. Medium V-shaped ears carried low and close to head. Short, stout neck

but oblique shoulders. Ribs flat-sided. Chest deep.
Straight, broad loin, slightly sloping to tail.
Double dewclaws on each hind limb. Feet close cupped.
Tail well feathered, carried low but rising high over the back when alerted.
Coat weather-resistant with fine white undercoat and thick outer coat, straight or wavy.
Has a rolling ambling gait but according to experts the dog should not 'roll in its skin'.

THE ROTTWEILER

A tall, powerful dog, active and free to manoeuvre. Bold and courageous. Head medium in size, broad between ears with marked occiput. Well arched zygoma. Moderate wrinkle when attracted. Deep muzzle equal in length above and below stop with the skull. Well developed black nose and nostrils. Almond eyes, dark brown. Smallish ears set high and lying flat above cheek.

Scissor bite. Black flews, not very prominent.

Neck fairly long, strong and rounded, slightly arched. Sloping shoulder and tight elbows.

Legs muscular straight and well boned. Pasterns sloping a little.

Chest broad and deep and ribs well sprung. Length from brisket to ground equals that from brisket to wither. Body only slightly longer than total height.

Upper thigh broad and fairly long. Hocks and stifles bent slightly so that hind limb is not completely vertical.

Coat consists of top and undercoat, of medium length, coarse and flat.

Colour black, with tan or mahogany brown markings on cheeks, muzzle, chest and legs, over both eyes and the area beneath the tail.

Size, males up to 27 inches; females up to 25 inches.

Beware of the roach and sway back, cow hocks, excess of coat, white markings and bad temper.

ST. BERNARD

The Standard records an expression of benevolence, dignity

and intelligence. Movement is most important and in many specimens the hind action is faulty.

The head is massive, the circumference exceeding twice the length of the head, with great length between the eye and the lower jaw. Stop abrupt and brows elevated with skull rounded on its upper aspect. Muzzle from stop to nose wide and flat. Eyes relatively small, deep set and dark. Lower eyelid droops showing haw. Ears smooth and medium in size hanging over cheeks. Mouth level. Thick slightly arched neck with dewlap.

Shoulders sloping. Legs straight and well-boned. Back broad and straight, good spring of ribs. Wide loin. Hocks and stifles bent, muscular thighs. Large, compact feet, well arched. Dewclaws removed.

Coat in Rough specimens dense and flat, fuller around neck and thighs. Smooth specimens have a flat coat slightly feathered on legs and tail.

Colours: organge, mahogany-brindle, red-brindle, white. Patches of any of these colours. Usually white blaze. May be a white collar, white chest, white forelegs and tail-tip; black shadings on face and ears. Fawn or self-colours are objected to. The larger the better so long as quality and symmetry are maintained.

SAMOYED

An alert, active and affectionate dog. Must have the characteristics of a draught dog. Body not too cobby nor too long but muscular with deep chest and well sprung ribs. Legs moderately long, carried well below chest to enable dog to travel at speed. Hocks and stifles should be well bent but the feet should not be carried far behind the body. Head, typical Spitz in type. Coat long on body and on the tail which is carried gaily over the back with a heavy plume.

Colour: white, white-and-biscuit, or cream. A white should have black eye rims, lips, and nose with very dark eyes.

SHETLAND SHEEPDOG

A miniature Rough Collie with some differences.

Colours: tricolours have intense black on body with rich tan markings. White markings may be a blaze, collar, chest frill, legs, stifles and tail tip. Wolf and grey colours barred. Sables may range from gold to deep mahogany. Blue Merles may be a clear silvery blue marbled with black. Heavy black markings are undesirable. Tan markings may appear on brows, cheeks, legs, stifles and beneath tail. Some white markings are preferable but not essential. Black and white and black and tan are acceptable. The white should never predominate in coat colour.

Gait must include speed with smooth, level action. No pacing, plaiting, rolling or up and down body movements.

WELSH CORGI (CARDIGAN)

An alert very active dog with a foxy expression and a body one yard long from tip of nose to tip of tail.

Skull wide and flat between ears, tapering towards eyes and domed. Length of muzzle is about three inches.

The Cardigan differs from the Pembroke Corgi in having a slightly longer head with a convexity of the skull making the ears seem wider apart. In many Cardigans the ears are wider at the base and generally larger than in the Pembroke. The jaw is a little less pointed than that of the Pembroke.

The Cardigan body is longer with more muscular loins. The tail is 10 inches long and generally carried low. The forelimbs usually show a little curvature. Coat shorter. May be brindle or black with white, fawn or red markings or blue merle (with silver-coloured eyes).

PEMBROKE CORGI

A bold little dog in a compressed space, alert and active. Not always friendly with strangers.

Head foxy, skull wide and flat between ears. Slight stop. Jaw tapers to a finer point than in the Cardigan. Length of foreface to that of skull is as 3 : 5. Ears, pricked and medium in size, slightly pointed. A line from nose to ear tip would pass through the eye. Eyes round and of medium size, hazel in colour. Bite level or scissor.

Neck should be fairly long, sloping shoulder. Forelegs short and *straight* (unlike the Cardigan). Tight elbows. Legs boned down to the feet with strong, only slightly sloped pasterns.

Body of medium length with well-sprung ribs and level topline. Chest full and deep, below elbow level. Hocks and stifles straight. Feet oval with two central toes slightly in advance of the others.

Tail: naturally short or docked.

Coat dense but not wiry. Colours: self in red, sable, fawn, black and tan or with white markings on legs, chest and neck. Some white on head and forehead permitted but never to produce hound markings or a Piebald or Skewbald effect.

UTILITY GROUP
BOSTON TERRIER

A breed relying largely on colour and markings but with a high degree of intelligence. A short-faced dog with erect ears bred by the Americans from the English Bulldog, the Old English Terrier and the French Bulldog.

Head short, square and domed on top. Well-defined stop and short square muzzle. Full, dark eyes. Ears a little smaller than in the French Bulldog.

Neck fairly long and slightly arched, body compact. Legs straight and moderately wide apart, pasterns short and strong. Tight elbows. Good deep chest, shoulders sloping, back short. Short loins, rounded rumps, flanks very slightly cut up.

Tail set on low, short, fine and tapering. Straight or screw, carried low or level.

Colour: brindle, with white markings though black and white markings are accepted. A white blaze over head, collar, breast, part or whole of forelegs and hind legs below hocks, are ideal.

Weight not above 25 lbs; middleweight 15 and under 20 lbs; heavyweight, 20 and under 25 lbs.

Objections: Solid black, black and tan, liver or mouse colour. Dudley nose, docked tail. Head too long, butterfly nose. Weak jaw showing turn-up. All white colouring.

BULLDOG

A smooth, low set dog with characteristic head and a pear-shaped body.

Head. As large as possible. Its circumference in front of the eyes should equal the height of dog at the shoulders. Very high from corner of lower jaw to apex of skull. Head should appear very high but short from nose to rear end of skull.

Frontal bones very prominent, broad and square, with a very deep stop. From the stop a wide, deep furrow extends up centre of head to its apex. The skin of the head is deeply wrinkled.

Muzzle short, broad and turned upwards and very deep from eye corner to mouth corner. Nostrils large, wide and black, with a well-defined vertical straight line between them. Flews, thick and hanging completely over the sides of the lower jaw, joining the under lip in front to completely cover and hide the teeth. The lower jaw projects well in front of the upper and is turned upwards. The eyes are set high on the head and very wide apart. Round in shape, of moderate size, neither deep-set, nor prominent, as dark as possible and showing no white when looking forward. Ears set high as wide apart and as far from the eyes as possible. 'Rose ears', small and thin.

Mouth should carry six incisors above and below in a straight line, the two halves of the lower jaw being quite symmetrical.

Neck not overlong, thick, deep and strong shoulders deep and inclined, very muscular, giving a wide brisket well let down between the forelegs. Ribs well-rounded, the front part of the body much heavier than the hinder end. Forelimbs well apart, heavily boned and straight, not bandy, with front feet turning slightly outward. Feed round and compact, with high prominent knuckles. The tail set on low, jutting straight out then turning downwards, thick at root and tapering to a point.

Coat fine and smooth, not wiry.

Colour whole, with or without black mask and muzzle or practically any whole colour barring Dudley, black and black and tan. Approximate weight: dog, 55 lbs; bitch, 50 lbs.

CHOW CHOW

An active short-coupled dog with tail carried well over back.

Head flat, broad, little stop, filled under eyes. Muzzle broad throughout and shorter than skull above it. Large black wide nose (except in creams and whites where a light nose is permissible but a dark preferred). Eyes dark, small, almond shape, a little sunken. Must be free from active entropion. Light eyes permissible in blues and fawns. Ears erect small, thick and rounded at tips, carried well forward over eyes and wide apart, producing a 'scowl'. Tongue, flews and roof of mouth, black. Scissor bite. Neck slightly arched and powerful.

Sloping shoulders. Straight forelegs. Chest broad and deep. Hocks and stifles perfectly straight. Small round cat feet. Rather coarse outer coat with soft woolly undercoat. Colours: whole black, red, blue fawn, cream or white, no patches or parti-colours.

DALMATIAN

A well-balanced muscular dog able to trot fast.

Head fairly long, skull flat and fairly wide between ears. Definite stop with skull and foreface on two levels. Long powerful square muzzle, tight lips. Nose black in black spotted, liver in the liver spotted. Ears set rather high, moderate size, wider at base, tapering to a point, carried close to head. Should be spotted rather than whole coloured. Eyes moderately wide apart, round. Black rim around eyes, or liver in liver spotted. Scissor bite.

Neck fairly long arched, light and tapering, without throatiness. Sloping scapula and straight forelimbs boned to the feet, with slight swing at pastern.

Body: Chest deep and not over-wide. Ribs carried well back. Well marked wither, level back, slightly arched muscular loins. Strong second thigh with well bent stifles and hocks. Tail down to hocks, inserted neither too high or low, carried with slight upward curve, but never fully curled. Cat feet and black or white or liver and white nails according to variety.

Great freedom of movement with long strides both fore and hind.

Coat short, hard and dense, sleek and glossy. Spots of dense colour which do not run together, size 1-2 inches diameter with clean edges and well distributed. Spots on body larger than on limbs. Black and liver spots must not appear on same dog. Dogs, 23-24 inches. Bitches, 22-23 inches.

FRENCH BULLDOG

A well-proportioned, active dog of Bulldog type but smaller and lighter.

Head large, broad and square, nearly flat between ears. Forehead domed and wrinkled. Muzzle broad and deep, lower jaw slightly undershot and well turned-up. Thick lips, meeting and hiding teeth. Deep stop, nose very short, black and wide with open nostrils. Flews not exaggerated. Eyes round and dark, not pop-eyed. Bat ears, wide at base, rounded at tips set high and carried upright with fairly wide space between them.

Body cobby, muscular and rounded off. Deep brisket, a roach back and narrowing at the loins. Abdomen well cut up.

Hind legs longer than the fore thus raising the rump. Hocks not over-bent but set on low down. Tail short, thick at root and tapering, short and never gay. Fine smooth lustrous coat.

Colours: brindle, pied and fawn. Tans and blues unpopular. Brindles may carry a little white. In the pied dog the white exceeds the brindle. A fawn dog may be partially brindle but must have black eyerims and eyelashes. Weight: Dogs 28 lbs, bitches 24 lbs.

KEESHOND

A short compact body, alert carriage, fox-like head, small pointed ears and well-feathered curling tail carried over the back. Hair thick on neck forming a ruff. Short fine dense hair on head, ears and legs. Movement straight and sharp.

Head fox-like, wedge-shaped from above with definite stop. Muzzle not too long, tapering to a fairly sharp point. Eyes dark with pigmented spectacles. Ears small, erect, not too wide, but not meeting. Scissor bite.

Forelimbs feathered, straight, cream in colour with good bone. Hind-limbs feathered down to hocks which are practically straight. Feet round and cat-like. Tail tightly curled preferably with a double curl at the end, with white tip.

Coat dense and harsh, dense ruff and well-feathered, profuse trousers and soft thick, light-coloured undercoat. Coat not silky, wavy or woolly, and without central parting. Colour:

wolf, ash grey; not all black or all white. Markings should be definite. Height for dogs, 18 inches; bitches, 17 inches.

POODLES

These include Standard Poodles, over 15 inches high, Miniatures from 11 to 15 inches. Toys up to 11 inches. The three types are identical in show characteristics apart from size.

Head long skull, narrow with slight occiput. Moderate stop. Foreface built-up below eyes, cheeks flat. Foreface fairly long and tapering. Lips tight fitting. Chin well-defined but not protruding. There must be a full set of teeth, six incisors above and below and a full set of four premolars above and below on either side. Rather long neck terminating in a well-inclined shoulder. Chest deep and ribs well rounded. Back short and slightly hollow. Loins broad and muscular. Thighs well formed with well-bent stifles and hocks close to ground, both hind legs parallel. Tail set on rather high but carried near level.

Very profuse, dense coat of harsh texture. All short hair close, thick and curly. All solid colours, pigmented spectacles and lips and toenails. Browns may have dark amber eyes, dark liver nose, lips, eyerims and toenails. Apricots to have dark eyes with black points or deep amber eyes with liver points.

Action must be straight and free, a fairylike stride in front with feet lifted slightly from the ground. Strong propulsion from behind.

SCHIPPERKE

Normally jet black, other whole colours have appeared: chocolate, dark blue and red. White is forbidden in the under-coat.

The head is more foxy than in any other Spitz breed. Wide skull between medium erect ears. Muzzle medium length, gently tapering with little stop.

Neck fairly short making the shoulders appear a little steep and broad. Deep brisket. Belly a little tucked. Hindquarters much finer than the fore portion. Legs straight in front and behind. Tail absent or docked.

Coat abundant, dense and harsh. Smooth on head, ears and legs but erect and forming a mane around the neck with a culotte on the back of the thighs.

Weight from 12 to 16 lbs.

SCHNAUZER

A medium sized robust dog with a beard, a hard wiry coat and a good undercoat, in pepper and salt colours or whole black, though a small white spot on breast is permissible. There are two sizes: dogs 19 inches, bitches 18 inches, and miniatures 14 inches in dogs and 13 inches in bitches.

The head is strong and elongated narrowing from ears to eyes and from there to nose tip. Broad between ears with flat creaseless forehead and comparative absence of cheeks. Medium stops and prominent eyebrows with fringes. Moustaches are heavy. Muzzle about equal in length above and below the stop. Ears erect and pointed.

Chest broad and deep with visible breastbone between elbows. Belly rising gradually to the groin. Limbs straight and well-boned. Moderate stifle and hock flexion. Feet short, round, well arched.

Tail docked to 3rd joint, set on high.

There is a miniature variety identical apart from size.

SHIH TZU

Head wide between eyes, broad and round. Hair falls downward over eyes and upward from the nose, the so-called chrysanthemum effect. Pronounced stop and heavy moustaches. Muzzle should be one inch long and pigmented. Level or slightly underhung mouth. Teeth must not show. Eyes large, dark, but not protruding.

Body longer than height at withers, well-coupled. Broad deep chest, level back and inclined shoulder. Tail heavily plumed and carried gamely over back. Forelegs short, straight and muscular. Hindlegs only slightly bent and parallel from behind.

Coat long and dense with good undercoat, straight and not curly.

All colours permissible especially with a white blaze and white tail tips.

Weight 9-16 lbs.

TIBETAN APSO

In a general way somewhat resembling the Shih Tzu with important differences. The chrysanthemum effect is not apparent and the muzzle is longer and straight. The length from tip of nose to eye equals one third of the distance from nose to end of skull. A squared-off muzzle is objectionable.

Colours: golden, sandy, honey, dark grizzle, slate smoke, particolour, black, white or brown. Golden or lion-like colours preferred.

Dogs, 9-10 inches at shoulder; bitches slightly smaller.

THE TERRIER GROUP

It is necessary when judging Terriers to recognise true Terrier type. A number of breeds are constructed much on the same lines with minor differences. A few, the achondroplastic breeds, are short-legged, and live close to the ground. These include the Scottish Terrier, the Sealyham and the West Highland.

The Airedale, Fox Terriers, Irish Terriers, Kerry Blue, Lakeland Terriers, and the Welsh Terriers rely upon sound Terrier conformation with individual differences.

The conformation includes a sloping shoulder, good length of neck, typical head, straight forelegs set well forward so that when standing on the lead the dog appears to rest on the front pads of the feet rather than upon the hinder heart shaped pad.

The back is straight and usually equal in length with height at the shoulder. The ribs are deep and inclined to flatness rather than to undue curvature.

The coat is made up of a fine close undercoat and an outer coat of longer hairs which may be wiry or soft according to breed requirements.

THE AIREDALE TERRIER has a long flat skull, not broad between the ears, narrowing to the eyes. There is very little stop and no wrinkling. The face is filled below the eyes with a strong foreface, devoid of cheeks. The lips fit tightly over the teeth. The eye is dark, small and does not show prominently. Ears, V-shaped with side carriage, not too large and neatly folded, never hanging limply at side of head. Scissor bite. Neck, fine but muscular, moderately long and well held-up.

Shoulders, forelimbs and body typically terrier, with little space between ribs and hips. Hindquarters not drooping, hocks and stifles well bent and parallel from behind. Small round compact feet. Coat, hard, dense and wiry. Body black or dark grizzle. Head, ears and limbs tan. Dark markings on each side of skull.

Height: 23-34 inches, dogs. 22-23 inches, bitches.

THE BEDLINGTON

Built more on whippet lines with distinctive mincing gait, a tendency to roll slightly at the trot though this disappears during the gallop, and the dog is capable of great galloping speed.

Head. Skull narrow but deep and rounded. Profuse silky topknot nearly white. No stop. Tendency to Roman nose but not exaggerated, the line from occiput to nose being continuous. Filled beneath eye. Close fitting lips without flews. Black noses in Blues and Black and Tans. Brown nose in Livers. Teeth level or pincer jawed.

Neck long, narrow near head, deep at the base, without throatiness, well lifted up from shoulders with head carried high. Ears moderate sized, set low, lying flat on cheek. Covered fine hair with white fringe at tip. Ribs not hooped inclined to flatness. Chest reaches down between elbows. Back roached and loin arched. Muscular galloping quarters. Hocks and stifles well bent. Tibia of good length.

Long hare feet with thick, tight pads. Tail moderately long, thick at root, tapering to a point. Never raised above back level. Coat thick and linty, not wiry.

Colour: blue, blue and tan, liver or sandy.

Height: 16 inches at shoulder. Weight: 18-23 pounds.

FOX TERRIERS

The Wire and Smooth should be identical beneath their coats. Typical Terrier conformation.

Head. Skull flat, moderately narrowing to eyes. Very little stop but a noticeable dip in profile between forehead and upper jaw. Cheeks flat. Jaws strong and neat, the distance between nose and stop being equal to or greater than from stop to occiput. Eyes small, dark, round and not prominent. The typical eye is described as 'varminty'. Nose jet black. Neck long, clean and muscular filling neatly into well-inclined shoulders. Ribs not too curved carried well back. Strong loin with stiff tail set high and carried straight and erect, not leaning too far forward. Forelimbs straight as posts, hind limbs bent at stifle and hock but the hindfeet should not rest far behind the level of the seat bones.

Weight: Bitch 15-17 lbs; Dog 16-18 lbs.

Colour: White predominates. Brindle, red, or liver markings objectionable.

IRISH TERRIER

A little more racy in build and considerably larger than the Fox Terriers and capable of fast speeds.

Head long, flat on top and narrower between ears otherwise similar to above. Ears carried high and neatly V-folded, the top of the fold, well above skull level. Coat hard and wiry and whole-coloured usually bright red, red wheaten or yellow red. A speck of white on chest not to be penalised but must not appear on feet. Chest deep and muscular but not wide. Body a little longer than in the Fox Terriers.

The weight for a dog, 27 lbs, bitch 25 lbs. Height 18 inches.

KERRY BLUE TERRIER

Larger and heavier still, the Kerry Blue is a tough, game dog of definite Terrier type with a will of its own requiring discipline.

Head long and lean, flat over skull with slight stop. Strong jaw which is trimmed to give appearance of depth and squareness. Neck strong . Front straight down from underline of neck, well-boned straight forelegs with deep chest reaching down inside elbows. Straight back with well-muscled second thighs and well-bent stifles and hocks, the latter set low to the ground. Tail tapered and erect. A square dog in every sense.

Coat soft and silky, plentiful and wavy.

Colour: Any shade of blue with or without black points. Puppies may be tan or dark in colour up to 18 months. Dogs: 18-19 inches; bitches, a little less. Weight about 35 lbs.

LAKELAND TERRIER

About equal in size to the Fox Terriers, the main differences apart from colour are that the Lakeland is shorter in head, differs in ear carriage and its eyes are rather smaller and set less obliquely. Its ears are smaller and not set so high on top of the head.

Colour: black and tan, blue and tan, red, wheaten, grizzle, liver, blue or black. Small tips of white on feet and chest permitted. Mahogany or deep tan untypical. Coat dense and weather resisting, harsh with good undercoat.

THE WELSH TERRIER

Very like the Lakeland and sometimes mistaken the one for the other, quite an understandable error until they are side by side.

The head is wider between the ears than in the Fox Terrier. The jaws are rather deeper, the whole head being rather less refined. The jaw is longer possibly than in the Lakeland, and slightly heavier and wider. In the Welsh Terrier the ears point a little more to the outside and the tips lie at the lower edge of the cheek. In the Lakeland the ears point more forward so that the tips lie touching the outer corner of the eye. There is, of course, a difference in appearance which cannot be explained on paper but is appreciated by those who patronise either breed. Coat rather more abundant in the Welsh.

Colour: black and tan, or black grizzle and tan free from black on toes. Black below the hocks is a fault.

SCOTTISH TERRIER

A sturdy thick-set dog that could never be mistaken for anything else.

A very long head which enables it to appear narrow. Nearly flat on top lines without prominent cheeks. Large black nose. The line from nose to chin slopes backward. Neck thick but not too long. Ears fine in texture, pointed and erect. Eyes almond shaped, dark brown, fairly wide apart, set deeply. Scissor bite.

Sloping shoulder, brisket showing between and in front of fore legs which are short, straight and boned down straight pasterns.

Ribs well-rounded on a deep chest and carried well back. Back short and muscular. Good short coupling. Hindquarters immensely powerful, big buttocks. Muscular long thighs, well bent at stifle and hock. Feet fairly large, toes well arched. Tail moderately long with upright carriage, sometimes with a slight backward curve in its length.

Colour: black, wheaten or brindle. Two coats, the outer harsh and wiry.

Height: 10-11 inches.

SEALYHAM TERRIER

A short-legged, moderately lengthy, mainly white dog, free moving and active.

Head. Domed slightly and wide between ears. Long powerful jaws. Rounded eyes, black, medium size. Ears wide at bend, lying over cheeks. Front straight down with short, straight forelegs, straight back with belly not far off the ground, powerful hindquarters and fairly short tail carried erect. Too much black a fault.

Coat, long, hard and wiry, reaching nearly to ground.

Weight: 18-20 lbs.

WEST HIGHLAND WHITE TERRIER

Nearly as low-to-ground as the Sealyham, very agile and varminty.

Head held higher than in the Sealyham on a rather longer neck. Skull slightly domed running almost parallel from ears to eyes. Jaws slightly shorter than skull, strong and level. The head is carried at right angles to the neck. Distinct stop between heavy brows. Eyes wide apart, separated by bridge of nose, and not over large or full. Ears small and erect, located a little to side of skull but facing directly forward. The lower canines lock in *front* of the upper canines. The upper incisors slightly overlap the lower incisors.

Neck fairly long merging into nicely sloping shoulders. Elbows tight to sides. Forelegs short and muscular, straight and thickly covered with hair. Very strong hindquarters. Hocks bent and set in under body and fairly close together. Forefeet larger than hind, round and covered with short hard hair. Pads and nails black. Tail, 5-6 inches, covered with short hair, no feather, straight and erect.

Coat pure white and doublecoated.

Size, 11 inches at withers.

BORDER TERRIER

A small working Terrier able to keep up with a horse, go to ground and swim if necessary.

Head, otter-like, broad skull, short strong muzzle, black nose preferred but liver or flesh colour accepted. Dark keen eyes, small V ears carried over cheek. Scissor grip or level. Not too long a neck. Body a shade longer than square with a thick tapering tail set high up to six inches long. Plenty of daylight under belly. Straight front and almost straight hocks. Ribs should be capable of being spanned behind the shoulder by a pair of hands. Dog, 13-15½ lbs. Bitches, 11½-14 lbs.

NORFOLK AND NORWICH TERRIERS

Mainly alike apart from the ears, upright in the Norwich, pendant in the Norfolk. A rather Cairn-like medium size Terrier with fairly short legs. Skull wide and slightly rounded between ears, wide at base and pointed at tips. Rather large eyes, oval, deep set and very dark. Muzzle of medium length, scissor bite. Short back and well-sprung ribs. Well-bent hocks low set. Round feet well padded. Medium dock, not above back level.

Colour. Black and rich mahogany tan. Muzzle tan to nose. Nose and nasal bone area black. Small tan spot on each cheek and above each eye. Underjaw and throat tan. Front legs tan, and *inside* of hindlegs. Black thumb mark above feet. For full details see the Official Standard.

Height at shoulders, 16 inches dogs, and 15 inches, bitches.

CAIRN TERRIER

A fearless, gay, medium sized Terrier, shaggy and game. Well forward on front feet with strong quarters, deep ribs and as straight as possible in front in spite of a tendency to slight bow-legginess. The fore feet sometimes turn a little outwards.

Sloping shoulder, fairly long neck. Back of only medium length with straight topline. Strong hindquarters and undocked tail, not feathered and carried below back level.

Head foxy, broad skull but only medium length jaw. Stop and definite indentation between eyes with bushy brows. Small erect pointed ears, fairly wide apart.

Coat, double. Profuse, hard but not coarse outer coat and furry undercoat. A lot of hair partly covers face unless trimmed.

Colour: red, sandy, brindle or nearly black. Dark points are preferred.

Weight: 14 lbs.

BULL TERRIER

An elegant, large headed, smooth coated dog with pointed erect ears and low-carried tail.

Head long and bluntly wedge shaped. Built up beneath eyes with rather prominent cheeks but not too markedly so. Scissor bite. Broad straight forehead without stop. Muzzle tapers but remains very powerful. Nose bent downward at tip. Small, deep-sunken dark eyes set obliquely and almond-shaped. Neck long and arched somewhat without dewlaps. Sloping, muscular shoulders, short forelegs well-boned and straight. Thighs heavy, hindlegs straight with only moderate bend of hock. Short pasterns with compact, rounded well-arched toes.

Coat pure white with silvery lustre on white body with head markings of black, fawn, tan or brindle. Coloured Bull Terriers may be self red, black, brindle, or black and tan with or without white markings. Miniature Bull Terriers should be small replicas.

STAFFORDSHIRE BULL TERRIER

A medium sized, sturdily built, smooth coated Bull Terrier of any colour.

Head unlike that of Bull Terrier. Medium length with very heavy cheeks. A very broad skull. Ears small, rose or half-pricked. Muzzle of only medium length, rounded above and falling away in front of the eyes. These are preferably dark but may follow coat colour. Set to look directly forward. Scissor bite. Tight, clean lips. Strong short neck widening towards shoulders. Forelegs must be straight and wide apart with wide sternum. Level topline. Close-coupled. Well-sprung ribs. Body lighter at loins and rear. Strong second thighs, hocks and stifles bent. Strong, medium-sized feet. Tail low-set tapering to a point and carried down.

Weight: dogs 28-38 lbs; bitches 24-34 lbs.

Height at shoulder: 14-16 inches.

DANDIE DINMONT

A long, low Terrier with a large head complete with topknot carried well in the air, a somewhat roached back over the loins, short legs and a long tail, thick as the base and tapering to a point. The skull is broad between the small pendant ears and the muzzle is deep but only moderately long. The head is covered with light silky hair while the muzzle is covered with darker hair. The body is well rounded and deep between withers and brisket, which is a little prominent. The under line sweeps upwards to the groin in a graceful curve. The back is covered with dark hair. The legs in length compare reasonably and are straight and well-boned.

Colour: pepper or mustard. Pepper runs from a dark bluish-grey to a light silvery-grey. Mustards vary from reddish brown to pale fawn. The head and topknot are creamy-white. White feet are objectionable.

Length from top of shoulder to root of tail should not exceed twice the height, preferably one or two inches less. Approximate weight 18 lbs.

AUSTRALIAN TERRIER

A low-set Terrier, very compactly built somewhat on Cairn lines but smoother. Head long, skull flat, full between eyes. Soft top-knot, long powerful jaw and black nose. Small dark eyes. Ears pricked, small, high on skull, or dropping forward. Level bite. Long neck, straight front and well-inclined shoulder. Docked.

Straight coat of hard texture. Colour: blue or silver-grey, tan legs and face. Blue or silver topknot. Height 10 inches. Weight 10-11 lbs.

SKYE TERRIER

A hairy low-set Terrier, fairly long in body.

Long head and powerful lengthy jaws well covered in long straight hair. Rather large prick ears rounded at apex. Body long and low. Back level. Rather flat sides. Broad shoulders, forelegs short, feet large and pointing forward. Short hind limbs without dewclaws. Tail pendulous ending in a curve. Double coat with soft hair on head and topknot. Tail feathered Ears surrounded with a fringe.

Colour: dark or light grey, fawn, cream or black. Black points. Nose and ears *must* be black.

Weight: 25 lbs. Height: 10 inches. Length: 41½ inches.

MANCHESTER TERRIER

The old Black and Tan English Terrier crossed with the Italian Greyhound.

A small graceful, smooth coated dog with V-shaped drop ears and medium length tail, undocked. Long wedge-shaped head with tapering muzzle, flat cheeks. Scissor bite with tightly fitting lips. Eyes small, dark and oblong. Long clean neck; short, slightly roach-backed body with arched loins and drooping croup. Chest, narrow and deep. Belly tucked up. Sloping shoulders. Straight forelegs, stifles bent and also the hocks, with a fairly long tibia. Hindlegs parallel from behind. Tail long and tapering. Semi-harefooted with arched toes.

Colour: jet black with mahogany tan markings.

Height at shoulders: Dogs 16 inches; Bitches 15 inches.

THE GUNDOG GROUP

ENGLISH SETTER

A friendly, elegant dog, a natural game dog.

Head. Long and lean. Well defined stop. Well defined occiput. Muzzle deep and square. The length is the same from nose to stop as from stop to occiput. Only slight flews. Nose black or liver according to coat colour.

Eyes very dark. Ears, moderate in length hanging in neat folds close to cheek. Level mouth. Long neck, arched at crest and clean cut to join the head. Not throaty.

Shoulders nicely sprung. Deep brisket with some width between shoulder blades. Ribs very well sprung. Body moderate in length, back short and level. Loins wide and slightly arched. Stifles and hocks well bent with muscular, lengthy second thighs. Feet close and compact and well covered by hair between the toes. Tail in line with back, medium length, scimitar shaped. Feathered at centre, tapering off at ends.

Coat slightly wavy but silky, black, lemon or liver with white or tricolour, flecking preferred to patches of colour.

Dogs, 60-66 lbs, height up to 27 inches. Bitches, 56-62 lbs, height up to 25½ inches.

GORDON SETTER

Head broader, deeper and heavier than in the English Setter; rounded between ears with prominent stop and visible occiput. Clear cut cheeks and clean tight lips. Scissor bite. Eyes bright and dark brown in colour. Ears set low on head, thin, medium size lying close.

Coat deep glossy black with rich, lustrous, chestnut-red markings. Black pencilling permitted on toes and under jaw. Short and fine on head, front of legs and tips of ears. Elsewhere of moderate length, with a fringe below belly extending forward up neck and throat.

Size: Males 26 inches; Bitches 24½ inches high.

IRISH SETTER

Racy in build and good natured. Famous for his beauty.

A large, well-coated, all red or rich chestnut dog with ears of moderate length set low and far back on the head. The head is particularly long, oval between the ears, the skull narrow and rounded, a well defined occiput, raised brows and a well-marked stop. Lips tight around mouth and the muzzle long, moderately deep and square at the front end. Nose large, black, dark mahogany or dark walnut. Eyes dark hazel or dark brown, not overlarge. Level mouth. Neck rather long but not too thick, somewhat arched and clean at the throat. Shoulders deep and sloped well back. Chest deep but with flat ribs in front, more curved behind. Wide powerful hindquarters with long tibia and well muscled thighs. Hocks and stifles well bent.

Feet small, firm and well-arched. Tail moderate in length, tapering to a point and carried level with or below the back.

POINTER, ENGLISH

The head is characteristic. Skull long and narrow with pronounced occiput. Nose and eye rims dark. The muzzle viewed in profile is slightly concave along the top giving a dish-faced appearance. Cheeks not full. Ears set high, hanging flat on side of face of medium size and thin in leather. Neatly filling lips without excessive flews. Eyes hazel or brown according to coat colour.

Neck long and widening at shoulders, sloping not erect. Higher at wither, sloping slightly to croup and stern. Tail long and tapering and carried horizontally. Chest deep and well-ribbed. Abdomen rises gently to groin. Forelimbs, straight, firm and lengthy. Hindlimbs long in tibia and well-bent so that the point of the hock lies well behind a perpendicular dropped from the seat bones. Coat fine, short and hard over whole body.

Colours: lemon and white, orange and white, liver and white, black and white, or self colour or tricolour.

THE RETRIEVERS

Those most commonly exhibited are the Flat-coated, Golden Retriever and the Labrador.

The Flat-coated is built on somewhat racy lines with a dense coat of fine quality, and texture as flat as possible.

All the Retrievers have relatively broad heads with a definite stop, the length from nose to stop and stop to occiput being approximately equal. The muzzle is powerful and wide, fairly deep and never snipy. The lips are neatly filling without pendulous flews. The tail is moderately short but in the Labradors it is distinctive being very thick near its base, gradually tapering towards its tip, shorter than in any other Retriever, and carrying a short, thick dense coat, free from feathering, giving it a rounded appearance described as the 'Otter' tail. The tail may be carried gaily, but should not curl over the back. In all Retrievers the ears are not over large, triangular, set high with a wide base and lying flat on the cheek with a rounded tip.

In the Flat-coats the first five or six ribs are rather flat, more rounded at the centre of the chest and less so nearer the flank. In the Goldens the ribs are generally more widely sprung and this also applies to the Labradors. It must be remembered, however, that in all breeds such as the Retrievers in which a flat, well inclined scapula is an essential, too great a width up to the fifth rib is apt to interfere with the freedom of the forelimb in its stride.

The Golden Retriever carries a flat or wavy coat with a deal of feathering and a dense water-resisting undercoat, in any shade of gold or cream, but never red or mahogany. A few white hairs on the chest are permissible.

THE LABRADOR RETRIEVER

In this breed the coat is close and short with a dense undercoat and is free from feather. Movement is important and this must be free both fore and aft.

The shoulder must be long and well-sloped to permit perfect front action while the loins must be wide and strong with well-turned stifles and hindquarters well-developed and set horizontally so that they do not slope downwards to the tail root. This applies also to the Golden variety and the Flat-coat though most Curly-coated Retrievers tend to slope slightly from the croup downward.

The colours in Labradors are generally black or yellow, but other whole colours are permissible. The coat should be free from white markings apart from a small white spot on the chest which is permissible. Any fleckings in the solid colouring of a coat are not appreciated.

The height in Labradors is up to 22½ inches, in Goldens up to 24 inches, and in Flat-coats 23 inches. The Curly-coated Retrievers may reach 27 inches.

THE SPANIELS

THE COCKER SPANIEL

Retains its popularity without effort. The head is characteristic. The distinct stop lies midway between the nose and the occiput which is well rounded but not accentuated. The skull is narrow and clean, slightly domed and nicely chiselled. The foreface is much deeper than wide and the lips descend far enough to provide delicate flews. It tapers slightly to its square-cut termination. The ears are long and wide, reaching the nose tip when held forward. They are set low on the head commencing at eye level, leaving several inches of dome above their point of origin. Eyes full but not prominent, never light in colour with tight rims. Level mouth with scissor bite. Neck fairly long and free from dewlap or throatiness. Fine sloping shoulders, brisket deep. Ribs rounded but not too much so beneath the scapula. Good straight back with strong loin, gently sloping from croup to tail which is set on fairly high, docked, and providing a merry side to side movement during all activities.

The forelegs are straight and lightly feathered of a length to enable the height from wither to ground to equal length from withers to tail root. Hind legs with muscular thighs and well-bent hocks, the leg below the hock being perpendicular when at rest.

Colours various. Self-colours may have a small spot of white on chest. Roans are popular. Weight 28-32 lbs. Height 15-16 inches.

THE SPRINGER SPANIEL

This is a larger variety weighing up to 50 lbs. It is higher on the leg than the Cocker and built on more racy lines.

The head may be very slightly broader than in the Cocker with a pronounced stop divided by a fluting between the eyes gradually dying away towards the occiput, which is not peaked. The ears are lobular in shape, set in line with the eye and of good length and width.

The body is rather longer than in the Cocker and not quite so square and compact.

Colour. Any recognised Land Spaniel colour, liver and white, black and white, or a tricolour with tan. Approximate height, 20 inches.

THE FIELD SPANIEL

A longer and rather lower-to-the-ground type, long coated with moderately long ears and a feathered tail. The head is characteristic being wide between the ears, with a well-developed skull and a prominent occiput. The muzzle is not correspondingly wide but equal in length to the skull portion with flat cheeks and very wide ears with the lower parts curling inwards and backwards and covered with feather. The neck is long and the body relatively longer than in the Springer in spite of being much lower on the leg. Tail carried in line with the back, fringed with wavy feather.

Coat flat or slightly wavy; abundant on chest, belly and behind forelimbs but short from hocks down.

Self-coloured by choice; black, liver, golden liver, mahogany red, roan, or any of these with tan markings over eyes, cheeks, feet and pasterns. Admixture of white is a fault.

Weight, 35-50 lbs. Height, about 18 inches.

CLUMBER SPANIEL

A heavy, massive dog, usually a slow mover, though classed as active.

Head large, square and massive, broad on top with marked occiput giving increased length and curve above and behind ears. Muzzle heavy, not overlong, with well-developed flews. Nose large and flesh-coloured. Ears large, vine-shaped and feathered tilting slightly forwards.

Body long and heavy, near the ground with wide chest and short, thick, straight forelimbs. Hindquarters very powerful, hocks well bent. Under surface of body nearly straight. Tail at back level, well feathered.

Colour. White with lemon markings. Freckled muzzled. Orange permitted but not desirable.

Weight: Dogs up to 70 lbs. Bitches up to 60 lbs.

WELSH SPRINGER

Red-and-white on the lines of the English Springer. Head rather narrower and lighter, ears smaller, pear-shaped and narrower at tips, with Setter-like feather. Rather heavier at

Fig. 31   Some Silhouettes

front end than at stern and more tucked up at flank. A very active dog.

Height: Dog must not exceed 19 inches and bitch 18 inches.

SUSSEX SPANIEL

A massive, but energetic dog, with a characteristic rolling gait. Head large and on two planes, the skull slightly curved from ear to ear being more horizontal than the foreface, $3\frac{1}{2}$ inches long, which dips down slightly from the stop. Occiput full and not pointed. Body not quite so heavy but resembling that of the Field Spaniel, though the neck of the Sussex is longer and inclined, so that the dog appears to possess a good 'forehand'.

Colour: rich golden-liver. Weight: up to 45 lbs.

IRISH WATER SPANIEL

Unique of its kind with a gait to match.

Rather large skull, high in dome and of fair width. Long, strong muzzle with a gradual stop. Skull covered with long curls and a topknot of long loose curls reaching the stop. Small, dark eyes. Long low-set ears, pendant in folds, and covered with long, twisting curls. Mouth regular, scissor bite. Neck, not overlong and set strongly into sloping shoulders, the head carried high upon it. Body deep at the shoulders with belly line tucked up considerably behind. The chest rather barrel-shaped. Powerful hindquarters, with long and well-bent stifles, very low set hocks. Large, round, spreading feet well covered in hair. Tail about seven inches, straight, thick at root, tapering to a point just above points of hocks. Close curls above but bare at its terminal portion.

Coat of dense, tight, crisp ringlets, naturally oily to resist water when swimming. Below hocks smooth in front but feathered behind.

Colour: rich dark liver with a purple bloom (puce-liver).

Height: Dogs 21-23 inches. Bitches 20-22 inches.

THE TOY GROUP

CAVALIER KING CHARLES SPANIEL

A very active, well-balanced dog with gay, free action. Head should be almost flat and without dome, between long ears set on high; well-feathered. Stop shallow.

The foreface from stop to tip of nose (black) is approximately one-and-a-half inches in length.

Eyes dark and set wide apart, rounded but not unduly prominent.

The muzzle tapers from back to front and the face is well-filled beneath the eyes.

Back short and level with well-sprung ribs with little space between the last rib and the stifle.

Forelimbs straight and well-feathered. Well-inclined shoulder. Tail may be docked, leaving two-thirds or left undocked. Well-bent hocks and stifles. Coat long and silky without curl. For permissible colours see Standard of breed. May be black and tan, ruby, Blenheim. Tricolour, or black-and-white (not popular).

Against. Domed head, deep stop, light eyes or nose, white markings in self colours.

Slack couplings. Cow hocks.

KING CHARLES SPANIEL

In contrast with the Cavalier the original King Charles differs in head, in being shorter on the leg and in weighing a quarter less than the Cavalier.

The head of the King Charles is large and domed between the ears, which are set on low and there is a pronounced stop. The black nose turns up to meet the skull and the lower jaw also turns upwards. The lips meet exactly without overlapping.

The dark eyes are set widely apart, are round and very large, providing a bright and intelligent expression.

Coats and colours are much as in the Cavalier but with rather more feather. For a fuller description of the colours permissible consult the breed Standard.

In the Blenheim the coat is white with evenly distributed chestnut red patches and a wide white blaze, with a chestnut spot about half an inch in diameter in the centre of the forehead.

Against. White hairs or patches in a black-and-tan. Lack of the "spot" in the head of a Blenheim. Too high on the leg. Tail carried over the back. Protruding tongue. Too long in back.

ENGLISH TOY TERRIER (Black-and-Tan)

The original English ratting terrier; fast alert and well balanced; compactly built throughout though fine in bone. Skull flat; head comparatively long, narrow and wedge-shaped with only a slight stop.

Ears erect (after the ninth month), set high on the head and well back on the skull, rather close together. They should be triangular with the tips slightly pointed and the apertures directed forward. When pressed down they should not quite reach the eye. The eyes are small and almond shaped, set obliquely and very dark in colour.

The mouth carries a level set of strong white teeth, the lower row tending to lean slightly forward with the upper row resting directly upon them so as to provide a level bite.

The neck should be long and slightly arched; the chest narrow but deep.

The scapula must be well inclined to give free front action.

The body outline should be neatly defined with no loose skin in sight.

The fore legs are straight and lightly boned.

The back slopes gently from wither to tail which tapers off from a stout root. It is set on low and should not reach below the hocks.

The coat is smooth, sleek and fine. Colour ebony black and chestnut tan.

For markings study the breed Standard.

Against. Snipy head. Too whippet-like in appearance. Eyes light, round or protruding, too small or too narrow.

Overshot mouth. Slack elbows. Height 10-12 inches.

The action should be long and striding, not hackney nor must there be short strides giving rise to a sloppy gait.

Hare feet. Gay tail carriage. Roached or dipped back. Bare skin areas. (Sixty years ago a great many members of the breed were hairless). Oversize. Any indication of a nervous disposition. Excessive hind angulation.

THE GRIFFON BRUXELLOIS

For. There are two varieties, rough and smooth, the latter being the Petit Brabancon.

Both are pert, squarely-built active little dogs, somewhat monkey-like, and far more heavily built than their general appearance suggests.

The head is wide between the ears, slightly rounded but in no way domed. Ears semi-erect and set high, as small as possible.

Nose black with large open nostrils, set high up on the face which is provided with a deep stop. From this the skull slopes gently to ear level.

The lower jaw is turned upward and is slightly undershot without the tongue protruding or the teeth visible. The whole produces a prominent chin which carries a distinct beard.

The eyes are large and round and the eyelids should be pigmented.

Neck only moderately long but slightly arched and moulded into inclined shoulders.

Back short and straight with its length equal to that from wither to ground.

Chest wide and deep. Strong loin and well-developed second thighs, with hocks and stifles slightly bent to give a strong forward drive. Small cat feet. Tail docked short and carried erect.

Colour red, black, or black and tan. Weight 6-11 pounds.

Against. Teeth visible, overshot, light eyes with unpigmented rims. Liver nose, curly coat, white patches, roached or hollow back, Hackney-like action, straight hocks. Body longer than high.

ITALIAN GREYHOUND

A miniature Greyhound not only reduced in size but also in slenderness and presenting perfection of symmetry, action and grace.

The skull is long, flat on the forehead with large dark eyes and delicate rose ears carried well back on the neck.

The neck is long and arched, melting into long well-inclined shoulders. The chest is deep and narrow with the belly well tucked up; the back arched from behind the withers, drooping at the hindquarters.

The limbs are straight, fine in bone terminating in long hare feet. The hocks and stifles are well bent, the second thighs muscular but not abnormally lengthy as in the English Greyhound.

The tail is long and fine, tapering to a point and carried low. The skin is fine with thin glossy satin-like coat. The colours may include fawn, cream, blue, black and fawn, and white pied, but black or blue with tan markings or brindle colours are not accepted.

The action is hackney-like with highstepping in front with hock flexion behind.

JAPANESE SPANIEL

A stylish little black-and-white or red-and-white dog with a profuse coat and a dainty high-stepping action with a heavily plumed tail carried over the back.

The term "red" includes all shades of sable, brindle, orange and lemon, in patches evenly distributed over the body, cheeks and ears.

The head is broad and big with a rounded forehead and a very short, wide muzzle. The eyes are set far apart, large with dark pupils and iris. The whites of the eyes must show at their inner corners to give the characteristic Japanese expression.

The nose is black and large in black and white dogs but may be brown in red and white.

The mouth is large and wide, neither under nor overshot. The tongue and teeth must not show. The ears are V-shaped, set on high, wide apart and drooping slightly forward.

The neck is rather short, the body wide in chest, short in back, thus producing a square outline.

The legs are straight and well-feathered with fine bone and long hare feet, also feathered. The tail is well-plumed, carried high over the back. The coat is straight, long and profuse, neither wavy nor curly, with a frilled neck.

Weights are frequently divided into "under or over 7 lbs." Small dogs are preferred.

Against. Flapping ears; pale eyes; too short in leg; tail carried low; cat feet; curly coat; insufficiently compact, narrow chest; bad mouth; lack of eye-white evident.

THE CHIHUAHUA

The smooth and rough varieties are identical apart from their coats. The rough variety has a soft, flat or rather wavy coat which should never be curly. The feet are feathered with long trousers behind, a ruff around the neck, with a long plumed tail.

Chihuahuas are cheeky little dogs, very active and quick on their feet.

The head has an apple-shaped skull with large, erect ears, wide at their bases, set far apart and protruding at an angle of 45 degrees from each side of the head.

A deep stop with a short tapering lean jaw; round, full eyes but not pop-eyed; preferably dark or ruby although light eyes are permitted in light-coloured dogs.

The mouth must be level with scissors bite.

The neck is slightly arched, of medium length, merging into lean, sloping shoulders which widen below in order to support straight forelegs, set well under the body.

The back is level, a little longer than the distance from withers to ground, doing away with any square-bodied appearance.

The tail is carried high over the back. It should be rather flat, widening in it's middle third, then tapering to a point. The feet are small with toes well split-up; not hare feet nor definite cat feet. Nails should be left fairly long.

The coat is smooth and glossy. Colour or colour mixture not restricted. Weight preferably between 2 and 4 pounds; the smaller the better.

MALTESE

A good natured and highly intelligent pure white dog, occasionally provided with light lemon markings. The coat is profuse, straight and of a silky nature which parts in the mid-line and falls on either side to the ground without impeding the natural free action. There is no undercoat.

The back is short producing a cobby little dog on rather short legs with a heavily feathered tail carried over the back but not gay during moments of enhanced activity.

The head is almost circular when viewed from the front with a wide, slightly arched forehead with long ears hanging close to the sides of the head, their heavy feathering mingling with the hair of the shoulders.

A pronounced stop divides the head into two portions equal in length.

The eyes are wide apart, large and dark with well-marked pigmentation encircling the eyelids.

The mouth is level with scissor bite.

The neck is moderately long but rather upright enabling the head to be carried level with the tail. It runs neatly into well inclined shoulders. The compact body has a level back and well-sprung ribs. The forelegs are short and straight with firm elbows; the hind limbs well angulated but not sufficiently as to carry the hind feet far behind the level of the seat bones.

Size: Not exceeding ten inches from shoulder to the ground.

Against. Mouth not level. Lack of eyelid pigmentation. Nose not completely black. Curly or woolly coat. Gay tail. Absence of a free striding action. Dishing or plaiting in front. Unpigmented foot pads.

MINIATURE PINSCHER

A square-bodied, well balanced, smooth coated Toy dog built on the lines of a miniature Hackney with it's characteristic gait. Head rather elongated and narrow without conspicuous cheeks. Muzzle not snipy with scissor bite.

Eyes of medium size, not slanting; as black as possible.

Ears may be erect or drooping but set on high and small and neat. Nose black, though silvers and blues may have self-coloured noses. Neck slightly arched without throatiness, fitting smoothly into sloping shoulders.

Chest a little flat at elbow level, widening out behind thus permitting free forelimb action. Body square with belly slightly tucked up. Rather wide across the hips. Back straight but gently sloping downwards from wither to tail root. Hind limbs quite parallel with nicely bent stifles and hocks. Straight forelimbs without too heavy bone. Cat feet with pigmented nails. Tail carried rather high but docked short.

Smooth lustrous coat. Colour black, blue, chocolate or solid red of various shades, with tan on cheeks, lips, lower jaw and throat with tan spots above the eyes and on the cheeks, lower halves of fore legs, inside of hind legs and under the tail, on lower part of hocks and feet which are cat-like. Black pencilling desirable on toes.

Slight white on chest is permissible but undesirable.

Height: 10-12 inches.

PAPILLON

There are two types of Papillon and in each case the head, from an exhibition standpoint, is of great importance.

In the Papillon proper, the ears are carried erect and spread obliquely like the wings of a butterfly.

In the Phalene (moth), the ears are completely drooped.

In either case the ears are rounded, set far apart and high on the back of the head thus emphasising the rounded outline of the skull. They should be heavily fringed.

The eyes are rounded, set low in the head and must not bulge. The lips are thin and light. Mouth has a scissor bite. The neck is of medium length, set into sloping shoulders. The chest must be deep but not overwide. The topline is level with plenty of length, being rather long in the loin.

Hindlimbs parallel with bent stifles and hocks. Dewclaws must be removed. Hare feet with tufts of hair prominent between toes.

Tail plumed, set high and carried over back with fringes dropping over side of body.

Colour white with patches of any colour bar liver.

Symmetrical head markings with narrow clearly defined blaze.

For a list of possible faults consult the breed Standard.

PEKINGESE

A proud little dog carrying himself like a miniature lion, but friendly and very intelligent.

Head massive with broad skull, wide and level between the ears, never dome-shaped. Eyes wide apart, large clear and prominent but never pop-eyed.

Nose short and broad, muzzle wide and wrinkled.

A very deep stop is typical, leaving a flat-faced profile with nose close up between the eyes with a firm underjaw.

Broad, heartshaped ears not extending below the muzzle, well feathered and carried close to the sides of the face.

Lips level and meeting closely without showing either tongue or teeth.

Back level and short with wide ribs. The hinder third is lighter in build than the front portion.

This front portion is cradled between the scapulae giving the appearance that the body is propped up on the fore legs.

Hindlimbs must not be too heavy, carried close behind without being cow-hocked.

Feet large and flat (not round), with straight pasterns.

The fore feet turn slightly outwards.

Tail heavily feathered and carried over the side of the back.

Coat long and straight with a profuse mane round neck and shoulders. Top coat rather stiff with profuse undercoat.

Heavy feathering on ears, legs, thighs, tail and toes.

Pekingese, when handled, are much heavier than their conformation suggests.

PUG

A square, blocky little dog, very condensed and very muscular.

Head large, round, but not apple-headed. It has a smooth surface free from indentations.

Muzzle short and broad but not upfaced. Large deep wrinkles on head. Eyes prominent and very dark in colour, round with a kindly expression.

Ears may be either rose or button, the latter preferred. They should be soft and thin and feel like velvet.

Body short and cobby with well-sprung ribs. Legs all of moderate length, carried well under the body.

Hind limbs strong and straight with feet carried beneath the body rather than behind it. Feet medium in size, not hare-footed nor small like a cat's. Nails black.

Tail curled as tightly as possible over the hip. A double twist is much admired.

Coat fine and soft and glossy, never woolly or curly.

Colour silver, apricot, fawn or black. There should be a well-defined black mask with black moles on cheeks. There should also be a black line running down the centre of the back from occiput to tail.

YORKSHIRE TERRIER

A terrier-like little Toy with a long coat parted in the middle of the back from nose to tail.

A strong little dog, active and well-proportioned.

Head rather small and flat on top with muzzle of medium length.

The coat on the head should be of a rich golden drooping over the side of the face, around roots of ears and on the muzzle where it is very long.

The tan on the head must not extend to the neck and nowhere must dark hair mingle with the tan.

Eyes placed frontally, dark, medium sized and not prominent. Rims of eyelids pigmented. Ears small and V-shaped, fairly close together, erect or nearly so, coloured rich deep tan.

The mouth must be even. A tooth missing from accident is not a fault.

Forelimbs a rich golden tan up to (but not above) the elbows.

Back level. Body short with good loin. Hindlimbs perfectly straight and a golden tan to above the stifle.

Feet round with black nails.

Tail docked and carried a little above back level, a darker blue than the body colour. Coat long and quite straight, silky and glossy. Colour, a dark steel blue (not silver blue), from occiput to root of tail, free from fawn.

Chest bright tan. All tan hair should be darker at it's roots and shading to light tan at it's tips.

Weight should not be above 7 lbs.

Addenda
FOREIGN BREEDS NOW BEING EXHIBITED IN BRITAIN

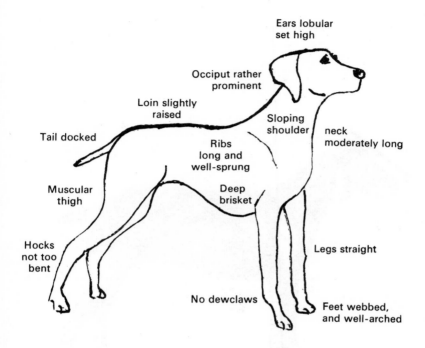

Ears lobular set high

Occiput rather prominent

Loin slightly raised

Tail docked

Sloping shoulder

neck moderately long

Ribs long and well-sprung

Muscular thigh

Deep brisket

Hocks not too bent

Legs straight

No dewclaws

Feet webbed, and well-arched

Coat grey, short, smooth and sleek.

THE WEIMERANER

A medium-sized dog, grey with light amber or hazel eyes. Has a rather awkward walk. Keen, fearless and friendly. Eyes may darken when dog is excited and the pupils dilate.

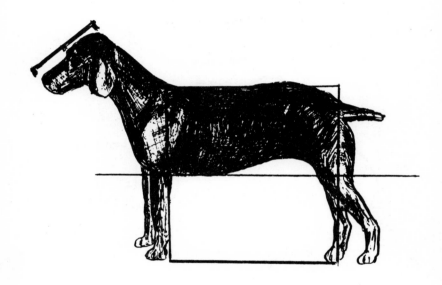

THE WEIMERANER
According to the Standard, the length of the body from the highest point of the withers to the root of the tail, should equal the measurement from the highest point of the withers to the ground. The measurement from elbow to ground equals that from elbow to highest point of the withers.

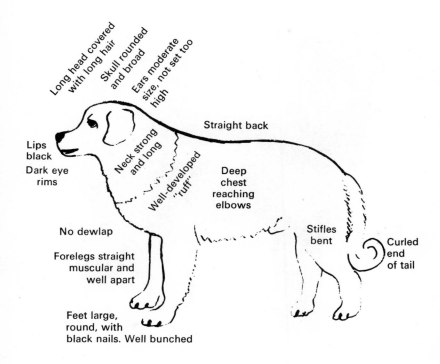

Long head covered with long hair

Skull rounded and broad

Ears moderate size, not set too high

Straight back

Lips black

Dark eye rims

Neck strong and long

Well-developed "ruff"

Deep chest reaching elbows

No dewlap

Forelegs straight muscular and well apart

Feet large, round, with black nails. Well bunched

Stifles bent

Curled end of tail

KUVASZ (KOO-WASS)
Hungarian Guard Dog
Height over 23 inches (dogs)   Height over 20 inches (bitches)

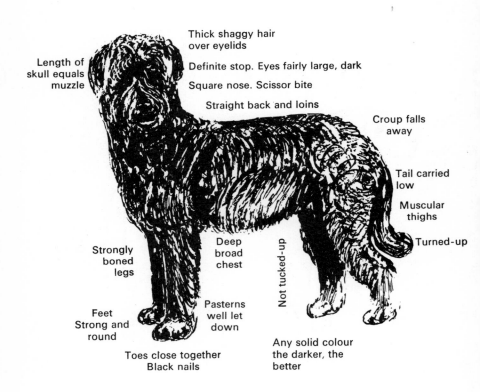

Thick shaggy hair over eyelids

Length of skull equals muzzle

Definite stop. Eyes fairly large, dark

Square nose. Scissor bite

Straight back and loins

Croup falls away

Tail carried low

Muscular thighs

Turned-up

Strongly boned legs

Deep broad chest

Not tucked-up

Feet Strong and round

Pasterns well let down

Toes close together
Black nails

Any solid colour the darker, the better

THE BRIARD
The shepherd dog of the Brie district of France.
Dogs, 24-26 inches   Bitches, 22-25 inches

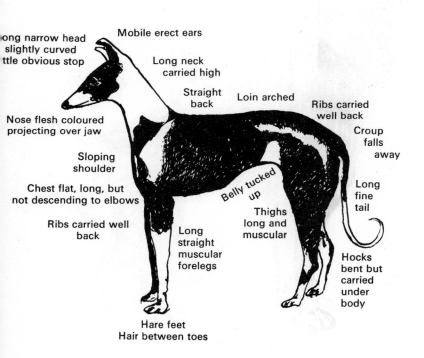

ong narrow head
slightly curved
ttle obvious stop

Mobile erect ears

Long neck
carried high

Straight
back

Loin arched

Ribs carried
well back

Nose flesh coloured
projecting over jaw

Croup
falls
away

Sloping
shoulder

Chest flat, long, but
not descending to elbows

Belly tucked
up

Long
fine
tail

Thighs
long and
muscular

Ribs carried well
back

Long
straight
muscular
forelegs

Hocks
bent but
carried
under
body

Hare feet
Hair between toes

IBIZAN HOUND (PODENCO IBICENCO)

Coat usually short but may be long. Colour: Red preferred. May be
all white or red and white mottled. Height: Dogs 23-26 inches,
weight 50 lbs. Bitches 22-24 inches, weight 42 lbs. An intelligent
all round sporting dog will catch and retrieve fur or feather.

THE FINNISH SPITY

A medium-sized prick-eared dog with a thick coat and a bushy tail, curled tightly and resting on one thigh. A thick muff around the neck and a bushy growth of hair behind the thighs. The head has a slightly domed skull, a clearly defined slope and a narrow muzzle tapering evenly to the nose. Eye medium size and dark. Chest deep and well ribbed above, tapering towards the breast bone. Back straight and short. Flanks tucked up. Limbs, strong and straight in front with well inclined shoulder. Hind limbs with hocks bent but feet carried close behind body. Colour dark red or fox red. Some black hairs and a little white on chest permissible. Height: Dogs $17\frac{1}{2}$-20 inches. Bitches $15\frac{1}{2}$-18 inches.

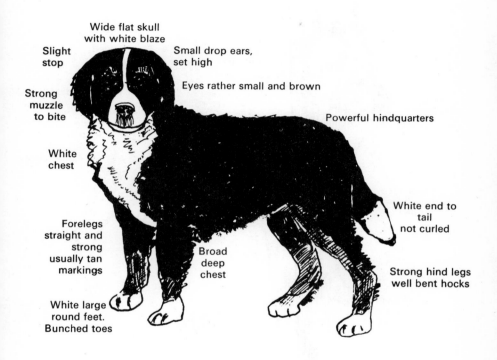

Wide flat skull
with white blaze

Slight
stop

Small drop ears,
set high

Strong
muzzle
to bite

Eyes rather small and brown

Powerful hindquarters

White
chest

Forelegs
straight and
strong
usually tan
markings

Broad
deep
chest

White end to
tail
not curled

Strong hind legs
well bent hocks

White large
round feet.
Bunched toes

BERNESE MOUNTAIN DOG
Height: Dogs 23-27 inches. Bitches 22-25 inches. Colour shining
black, tan and white. Coat long, soft and sleek.

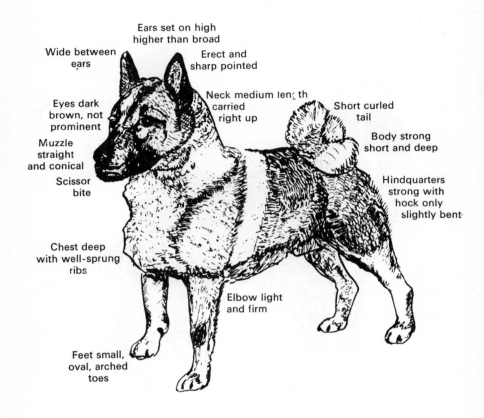

Ears set on high
higher than broad

Wide between
ears

Erect and
sharp pointed

Neck medium length
carried
right up

Short curled
tail

Eyes dark
brown, not
prominent

Muzzle
straight
and conical

Body strong
short and deep

Scissor
bite

Hindquarters
strong with
hock only
slightly bent

Chest deep
with well-sprung
ribs

Elbow light
and firm

Feet small,
oval, arched
toes

NORWEGIAN BUHUND
A medium size Spity.
Colour wheaten, black or not too dark red. Preferably whole colour
but white blaze, a narrow collar round neck and white spot on chest
or feet permissible.

THE PHARAOH HOUND

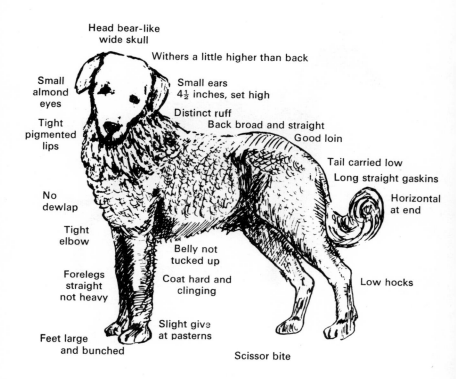

Head bear-like
wide skull

Withers a little higher than back

Small
almond
eyes

Small ears
$4\frac{1}{2}$ inches, set high

Tight
pigmented
lips

Distinct ruff

Back broad and straight

Good loin

Tail carried low

Long straight gaskins

No
dewlap

Horizontal
at end

Tight
elbow

Belly not
tucked up

Forelegs
straight
not heavy

Coat hard and
clinging

Low hocks

Slight give
at pasterns

Feet large
and bunched

Scissor bite

THE MAREMMA SHEEPDOG

Dogs: weight 75-95 lbs., height 25-28 inches. Bitches: weight 65-85 lbs., height 23-26 inches. Pyreneean massweness to be avoided.

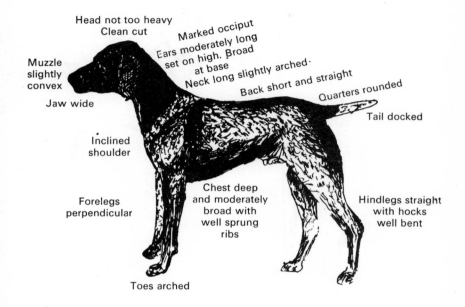

Head not too heavy
Clean cut

Marked occiput

Ears moderately long set on high. Broad at base

Muzzle slightly convex

Neck long slightly arched.

Back short and straight

Quarters rounded

Jaw wide

Tail docked

Inclined shoulder

Forelegs perpendicular

Chest deep and moderately broad with well sprung ribs

Hindlegs straight with hocks well bent

Toes arched

GERMAN SHORT-HAIRED POINTER

Coat short, dense, coarse and hard. Colour: light or dark brown, with or without markings; white with brown patches or spots, black and white or black tan and white.

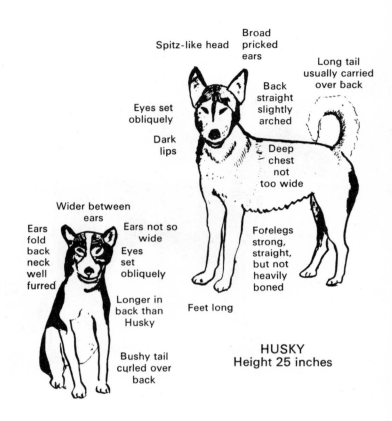

Spitz-like head

Broad
pricked
ears

Long tail
usually carried
over back

Back
straight
slightly
arched

Eyes set
obliquely

Dark
lips

Deep
chest
not
too wide

Wider between
ears

Ears not so
wide

Ears
fold
back
neck
well
furred

Eyes
set
obliquely

Forelegs
strong,
straight,
but not
heavily
boned

Longer in
back than
Husky

Feet long

HUSKY
Height 25 inches

Bushy tail
curled over
back

MALAMUTE
Height 21-25 inches

VIZLA
Hungarian Pointer
Up to two feet high and a beautiful pale yellow with short and glossy coat.

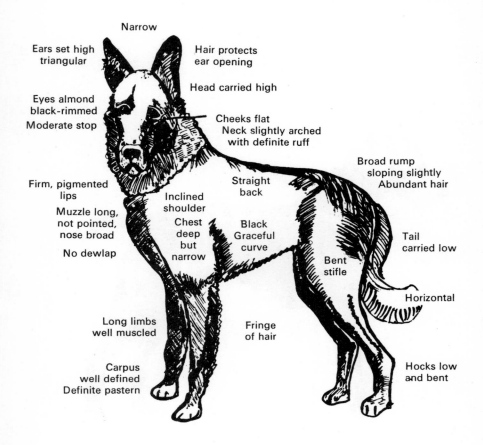

Narrow

Ears set high
triangular

Hair protects
ear opening

Head carried high

Eyes almond
black-rimmed

Moderate stop

Cheeks flat
Neck slightly arched
with definite ruff

Firm, pigmented
lips

Straight
back

Broad rump
sloping slightly
Abundant hair

Muzzle long,
not pointed,
nose broad

Inclined
shoulder

Chest
deep
but
narrow

Black
Graceful
curve

Tail
carried low

No dewlap

Bent
stifle

Horizontal

Long limbs
well muscled

Fringe
of hair

Carpus
well defined
Definite pastern

Hocks low
and bent

GROENENDAEL

Colour black. Limited white on chest, tips of hind toes and between
pads. Slight frosting on muzzle permissible. Coat thick and plentiful.
Height at withers: Dogs 24 inches. Bitches 22 inches. Length
withers to pelvis 16 inches. Total body length 24½ inches. Depth of
chest 12 inches.

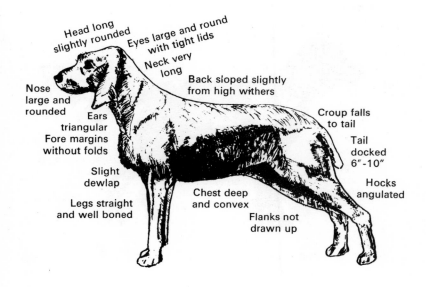

Head long
slightly rounded
Eyes large and round
with tight lids
Neck very
long
Back sloped slightly
from high withers
Nose
large and
rounded
Ears
triangular
Fore margins
without folds
Slight
dewlap
Legs straight
and well boned
Chest deep
and convex
Flanks not
drawn up
Croup falls
to tail
Tail
docked
6"-10"
Hocks
angulated

SPINONE (Italian)

Colour white, orange or brown markings permissible. Up to $27\frac{1}{2}$ inches high. Weight 62-70 lbs. A big dog with rough coat and long ears, docked. Length from shoulder joint to seat bone equals height from wither to ground. Dense, harsh top coat, soft under coat. Hair on head eyebrows and cheeks fairly long.

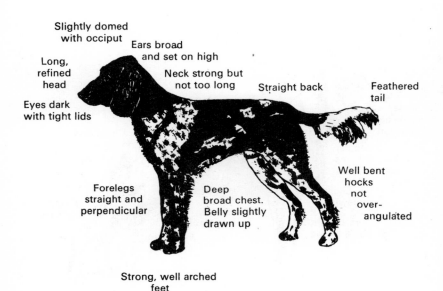

Slightly domed
with occiput

Ears broad
and set on high

Long,
refined
head

Neck strong but
not too long

Straight back

Feathered
tail

Eyes dark
with tight lids

Forelegs
straight and
perpendicular

Deep
broad chest.
Belly slightly
drawn up

Well bent
hocks
not
over-
angulated

Strong, well arched
feet

THE MUNSTERLANDER (Large)

23-25 inches high. A smaller type also exists only 18-22 inches high. A long-coated black-and-white dog. Head black, long ears and feathered tail. Coat sleek and slightly wavy, limbs feathered. Large white patches on body, ticked.

Ears pointed,
erect

Coat smooth

Narrow
between ears

Tail sometimes
docked

Body about
square

Weight: 25-30 lbs.

Height: 18-20 inches

Colours:
Black-and-tan
Blue-and-tan
Red-and-tan
Red-and-fawn
Chocolate
Slate

KELPIE
The Australian sheepdog. Strongly established in Australia and has
bred true to type since 1870.

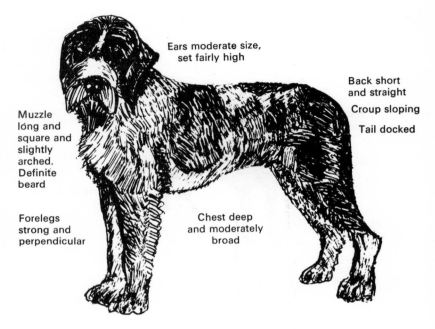

Head large and long,
not too broad or steep

Fairly long, strong neck

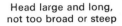

Ears moderate size,
set fairly high

Back short
and straight

Croup sloping

Tail docked

Muzzle
long and
square and
slightly
arched.
Definite
beard

Forelegs
strong and
perpendicular

Chest deep
and moderately
broad

POINTING GRIFFON

Height: Dogs 22-23½ inches. Bitches 20-22 inches. Shaggy coat,
steel grey with brown patches, white and brown, white and fawn or
all brown mixed with grey hairs. Top coat resembles fine wire.
Length of body in proportion to height = 10 : 9.

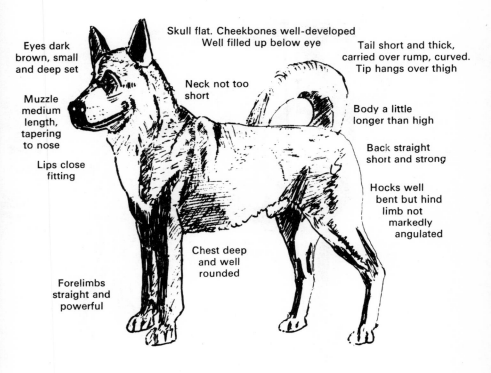

Head rather wide
between neat
prick ears

Skull flat. Cheekbones well-developed
Well filled up below eye

Tail short and thick,
carried over rump, curved.
Tip hangs over thigh

Eyes dark
brown, small
and deep set

Neck not too
short

Muzzle
medium
length,
tapering
to nose

Body a little
longer than high

Back straight
short and strong

Lips close
fitting

Hocks well
bent but hind
limb not
markedly
angulated

Chest deep
and well
rounded

Forelimbs
straight and
powerful

JAPANESE AKITA (Large Japanese Spity)

20-27 inches. A bold guard dog. The national dog of Japan. Top coat of medium length, harsh, straight and upstanding. Undercoat abundant, soft and wooly. May be red, white, wheaten, black, shades of grey, black and tan or brindle.

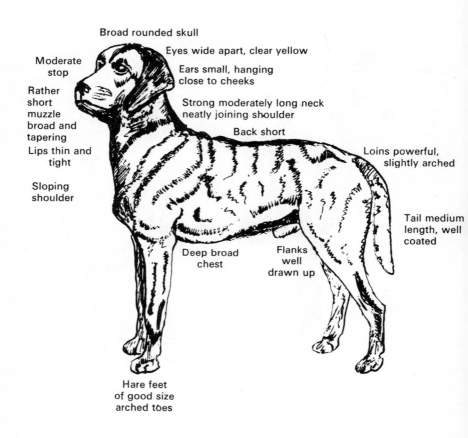

Broad rounded skull

Eyes wide apart, clear yellow

Moderate stop

Ears small, hanging close to cheeks

Rather short muzzle broad and tapering

Strong moderately long neck neatly joining shoulder

Back short

Lips thin and tight

Loins powerful, slightly arched

Sloping shoulder

Tail medium length, well coated

Deep broad chest

Flanks well drawn up

Hare feet of good size arched toes

CHESAPEAKE BAY RETRIEVER
A large strongly built dog weighing 60-70 lbs. Dogs 22-25$\frac{1}{2}$ inches high. Bitches 20-23$\frac{1}{2}$ inches. Coat not over an inch long, dense and thick. Colour brown to beige, white on chest and toes permissible.

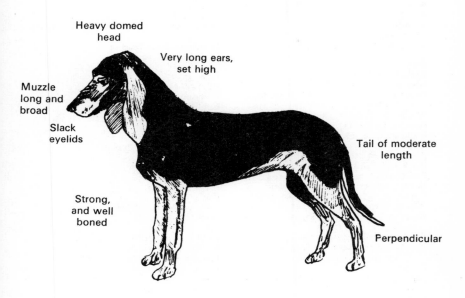

Heavy domed
head

Very long ears,
set high

Muzzle
long and
broad

Slack
eyelids

Tail of moderate
length

Strong,
and well
boned

Perpendicular

JURA HOUND (Swiss)

A long-bodied, short-coated hound. Must not exceed 18 inches high and not below 16 inches. Colour: Fawn or tan and black saddle, or black and tan. White spot on chest permitted.

Index

Index *(continued)*

Index *(continued)*